I0129556

Published by:

V&S PUBLISHERS

F-2/16, Ansari Road, Daryaganj, New Delhi-110002
☎ 011-23240026, 011-23240027 • *Fax:* 011-23240028
Email: info@vspublishers.com • *Website:* www.vspublishers.com

Branch : Hyderabad
5-1-707/1, Brij Bhawan (Beside Central Bank of India Lane)
Bank Street, Koti, Hyderabad - 500 095
☎ 040-24737290
E-mail: vspublishershyd@gmail.com

Follow us on: 🇹 f in

For any assistance sms **VSPUB** to **56161**
All books available at **www.vspublishers.com**

© **Copyright:** V&S PUBLISHERS
ISBN 978-93-814489-7-7
Edition 2013

The Copyright of this book, as well as all matter contained herein (including illustrations) rests with the Publishers. No person shall copy the name of the book, its title design, matter and illustrations in any form and in any language, totally or partially or in any distorted form. Anybody doing so shall face legal action and will be responsible for damages.

Printed at : Param Offseters, Okhla, New Delhi-110020

To Varun, my best friend and quizzing partner.

Contents

Preface

It has been quite a fun preparing questions for this book. Doing crazy things like pulling over to the kerb suddenly, just to make a note of a hoarding, noting something from the menu card of a restaurant, scribbling little facts from a book you are browsing through at a bookshop to frame different questions for the book....

'Why is this book different' might sound a cliché while reading the preface. If I may say so, it is different from other business quiz books available in the market in the sense that it tries to emulate the framing and variety of questions asked in business quizzes these days. Most of the questions in this book are workable ones and do not require any rote learning. Awareness about one's environment and an open mind are just sufficient to answer the questions. The length of some questions may be intimidating at some time but they have been designed in such a manner deliberately so that they are informative as well.

Although there is no dearth of resources like blogs and websites available these days but a compendium that has the best of the lot is the need of the hour. It will serve as a stepping stone for people who have started business quizzing and a delight for people who are stalwarts in the business quizzing arena.

Keep your eyes and ears open, and keep a tab on trivia. Look beyond the obvious.

Happy Biz Quizzing!!
–Saurabh Aggarwal

Section I
Questions

Advertising Saga I

Questions

1. Name the British-Indian novelist and essayist who is credited with the campaigns for Aero chocolate bars ('Irresistabubble') and the Daily Mirror newspaper ('Look into the Mirror tomorrow—you'll like what you see').

2. In 1932, he started selling Aga cooking stoves door-to-door. His success at this marked him out to his employer, who asked him to write an instruction manual 'The Theory and Practice of Selling the AGA cooker' for the other salesmen. Fortune magazine editors called it the finest sales instruction manual ever written. Identify the salesman.

3. Identify the pioneer of British advertising and the chairman of Benson who was behind slogans such as "Guinness is Good for You". He was also a founder member of the board of governors of the Cutty Sark.

4. She has been a traffic-stopper since 1967. Her wit, her sharp sense of humor and her unique style of analyzing current affairs have always been a subject of fascination. Towering over at all prominent landmarks of all major Indian cities, she has been attracting more eyeballs than even Bollywood bombshells. And at over 40, she continues to be envied by even the best in the industry. Who has been described?

5. Oliviero Toscani (an Italian photographer) is best-known worldwide for designing controversial advertising campaigns for which brand from 1982 to 2000?

> *"Give people a taste of Old Crow and tell them it's Old Crow. Then give them another taste of Old Crow, but tell them it is Jack Daniel's. Ask them which they prefer. They'll think the two drinks are quite different. They are tasting images." - David Ogilvy*

6. While working as an art director and designer in the Calcutta office of the ad agency D. J. Keymer, he read one of the best novels of

Bibhuti Bhushan Bandopadhyay. Later, based on that novel, he produced and directed a film of the same name (as that of novel) that became a milestone in Indian cinema. Identify the person being talked about in the question.

7. This company ran an advertising campaign in the early 1970s, simply showing a hand using this company's product to write the following 'mathematical' formula on a piece of paper:

$$\frac{(3.5G + \frac{v}{2})}{4(H_2O)^3} + 3(360°) = M$$

The result was that they received numerous inquiries by chemists, mathematicians, and physicists, asking for the meaning of the formula, as they could not figure it out. The formula is actually a humorous representation for the recipe of a martini. Apparently the campaign received one very critical letter asking "Who ever heard of a martini without an olive?" Which company ran the above campaign?

Cadbury launched a new in-house production company called "A Glass And A Half Full Productions" in 2007. It was responsible for an advertising campaign entitled Gorilla which was premièred during the season finale of 'Big Brother' 2007.

8. Which company developed the "Army Strong" campaign for the United States Army? It is a subsidiary of the Interpublic Group of Companies.

9. Which American businessman is often considered to be the founder of modern advertising? He is also known as a former owner of the Chicago Cubs baseball team.

10. He began working as a journalist, but left to work as a salesman so that it was easier for him to support his wife. He discovered advertising while working as a salesman, and began working with ad firm F Wallis Armstrong in 1916. He co-founded his own firm in 1923. He pioneered the systematic study of consumer preferences. His credo was "resist the usual". Name the person.

11. What portmanteau term is used to describe a newspaper or magazine ad resembling editorial in style and layout?

12. In September 1938, Harry Oppenheimer travelled from Johannesburg to New York City, to meet the president of N. W. Ayer. An N. W. Ayer copywriter came up with a caption which was scrawled on the bottom of a picture of two young lovers on a honeymoon. What was the caption? The caption was adapted by Ian Fleming as the title of his 1956 work, which also went on to become a movie.

13. He was born in Calcutta and moved to Paris in 1973. His successful work on Amnesty International was a turning point in his career. Following his dreams, he quit advertising and started his own design company, Shining Strategic Design. Who has been described?

The world's first television advertisement was aired on July 1, 1941 on New York's WNBT-TV. The 10-second ad for Bulova clocks and watches displayed a picture of a clock superimposed on a map of the United States accompanied by the voice-over "America runs on Bulova time."

14. Founded in 1982 in Oregon, it is an independently owned American advertising agency best known for its work for Nike. They also designed the Lance Armstrong's Livestrong yellow bracelet campaign to raise funds for cancer research. Name the agency.

15. Founded in Chicago in 1873, the agency was called Lord & Thomas until 1942, when Albert Lasker sold the firm to its three top managers – Emerson Foote in New York, Fairfax Cone in Chicago and Don Belding in California. Name the ad agency.

16. Which multinational advertising and communications company derives its name from a combination of the French word for advertising and the sound of the French 'six' to denote the year of the company's formation? It was started in 1926 by the founder of modern French advertising – Marcel Bleustein Blanchet.

17. According to David Ogilvy, there can be three types of brand names :
    (a) Names of men and women e.g. Ford, Campbell. These are memorable, difficult to copy and human.
    (b) Descriptive names like 3-In-One Oil, Janitor in a Drum. Such names start with sales appeal, but struggle with brand extensions.
    Identify the third one.

18. He worked as a journalist before starting work as a copywriter in 1917. In 1935, he founded his own agency. His philosophy was to create an image around the product, and to capture what he called the "inherent drama" of the brand. The Marlboro man was one of his most famous creations. Who?

19. Which agency was behind the historic campaign against the British Labour party, which was instrumental in Margaret Thatcher's election in 1980?

20. He was a legendary figure in the history of American advertising and directed ad campaigns such as "Think Small" for Volkswagen Beetle and "We Try Harder" for Avis Car Rental. Who is he?

Answers

1. Salman Rushdie
2. David Ogilvy
3. Bobby Bevan
4. Amul Girl
5. United Colors of Benetton
6. Satyajit Ray; the novel was Pather Panchali
7. Parker Pen Company
8. McCann Erickson
9. Albert Davis Lasker
10. Raymond Rubicam
11. Advertorial
12. A Diamond Is Forever; Harry Oppenheimer was the son of the founder of De Beers.
13. Shombit Sen Gupta
14. Wieden+Kennedy
15. FCB (Foote, Cone, & Belding)
16. Publicis. French word for advertising is 'publicité'
17. Meaningless names like Kodak or Kotex. He warns that these take years and many millions of dollars to endow with sales appeal.
18. Leo Burnett
19. Saatchi & Saatchi
20. William (Bill) Bernbach

✠✠✠

Advertising Saga II

Questions

1. The red apples placed on every receptionist's desk, an icon of a 'hand reaching for the stars' and a 'black pencil'. What do these signify?

2. This company was founded by brothers Maurice and Charles in 1970. They were noted for their campaign "Labor isn't working" on behalf of the Conservative Party before the 1979 UK general election. Which company was founded by the two brothers?

3. In 1953, Baskin-Robbins hired Carson-Roberts Advertising who recommended adoption of the famous "31" logo, the "31 flavors" strategy, as well as the pink (cherry) and brown (chocolate) polka dots and typeface that were reminiscent of the circus. What did Carson-Roberts Advertising eventually become?

4. What was created by the Leo Burnett advertising agency's copy-writer, Rudy Perz, as he was sitting in his kitchen in 1965, under pressure to create an advertising campaign? It was originally drawn by Martin Nodell and brought to life using stop motion clay animation.

5. The company was called Wire and Plastic Products, a maker of supermarket baskets. Its main attraction was that it was listed and could be acquired for less than a million pounds in 1985. The new owner made 15 acquisitions in 2 years launching the platform for a services giant that now encompasses some 250 companies. Name the person who acquired the company in 1985.

Volney B. Palmer opened the first American advertising agency, in Philadelphia in 1850.

6. Which advertising icon was named the second most popular American woman in 1945 by Fortune magazine?

7. A group of Clydesdale horses are used for promotions and commercials by which brewing company?

8. Which Paris-based design studio was hired to craft a new logo and corporate slogan for Britannia Industries Limited?

9. Which advertising agency was founded by a mining engineer – Ravi Gupta and its name is a derivative of a Sanskrit word that means three forms symbolizing – Creative, Marketing and Media?

10. Name the American advertising personality whose most typical ad is probably that for Anacin, a headache medicine.

11. After failing the first year of college, he ran away from home, and at 18, took up a job as a crop-sprayer across rural India. He founded an ad agency and also co-founded India's first private TV channel. In 1999, he sold the agency to the $5 billion Publicis Groupe, continuing as adviser for its Indian mergers and acquisitions. Name him.

12. The man who appeared in the ad was Baron George Wrangell, who was a Russian aristocrat with 20/20 vision, but the advertisement's creator, David Ogilvy, was inspired by a picture of Lewis Douglas, who had lost an eye in a fishing accident. Which company's ad has been described?

The term "Energizer Bunny" has entered the vernacular as a term for anything that continues indefatigably. Several U.S. presidential candidates have compared themselves to the bunny, including President George H. W. Bush in 1992 and Howard Dean in 2000.

13. Identify this male advertising model who wrote two bestsellers (one of them was titled 'Passport to Power') and was the wardrobe advisor to George W Bush (Senior).

14. Which company was originally founded by William James Carlton in 1864?

15. Which ad agency was founded by Hoshiro Mitsunga as Japan Advertising Limited and Telegraphic Service Co.?

16. He was a pioneer in the business of advertising. Under his leadership, JWT became a leader, not only in print advertising, but also in radio advertising and programming. Identify him.

17. He dropped out of Oxford, and worked as a chef and a salesman. He began his career in advertising at the age of 38, and went on to co-found his company. He attained legendary status, primarily due the iconic campaigns he created for Dove, Rolls Royce, Hathway shirts etc. Who?

18. Which company introduced the slogan 'Come alive! You're in the Pepsi Generation' in 1963? It is the first time a product is identified not by its own attributes but by its consumers' lifestyles and attitudes. Hammermill Paper Company is their oldest client.

Kirloskar Group once owned an industrial advertising company called Pratibha Advertising headed by Geetanjali Kirloskar.

19. In the years following World War II, advertising executive Leo Burnett was looking for a new image to reinvent the brand. Burnett's inspiration for this icon came in 1949 from an issue of LIFE magazine, where the photograph (shot by Leonard McCombe) and story of Texas cowboy Clarence Hailey Long caught his attention. Which icon was created by Leo Burnett?

20. Name the ad agency behind the 'Lalitaji' campaign.

Answers

1. Internal corporate symbols created by Leo Burnett
2. Saatchi & Saatchi
3. Ogilvy and Mather (O&M)
4. Pillsbury Doughboy
5. Martin Sorrell (WPP)
6. Betty Crocker
7. Anheuser-Busch
8. Shining Strategic Design
9. Trikaya Grey Advertising
10. Rosser Reeves
11. Ashok Kurien, founder of Ambience Advertising and ZEE TV.
12. C. F. Hathaway Company
13. William Thourlby, the Marlboro Man
14. JWT
15. Dentsu
16. Stanley Burnet Resor
17. David Ogilvy
18. BBDO
19. Marlboro Man
20. Lintas

✠✠✠

Auto Expo I

Questions

1.   The emblem of this German auto major symbolizes the amalgamation of this company with 3 other auto companies namely DKW, Horch and Wanderer. Identify the company.

2.   In 1931, this luxury automobile company was bought by Rolls-Royce secretly using a company named the British Central Equitable Trust. The true identity of the purchaser was not even known to this company until the deal was completed. The founder of this company was called "W.O" and was previously known for his successful range of rotary aero-engines in World War I. Identify this company.

3.   These are the taglines used by this auto major over the years:

   1974 – "Small car specialists for 40 years."

   1975 – "Oh! What a feeling."

   1976 – "Who could ask for anything more? You asked for it, you got it!"

   Identify the car maker from the taglines.

   🔅 *Volvo was the company which introduced the safety belts.*

4.   Which company's founder realising that an auto manufacturer with only one car line stood little chance of survival, brought together about 25 carmakers and suppliers within 18 months of the company's founding?

5.   The origins of this company go back to 1927 when designer Ferdinand Porsche who had created a number of expensive state-of-the-art cars, turned his attention to a simpler low end vehicle. In 1933, Adolf Hitler took an interest in Porsche's ideas. In 1937, a company was set up by the German Government to achieve a single purpose – create a cheap automobile for the masses. Identify the brand created by Ferdinand Porsche.

6. Which automobile company's founders wrote "Cars are driven by people. For this reason safety is, and must remain the guiding principle behind everything we do"?

7. Name the automobile marque started by Edsel Ford in 1939 and derives its name from the "messenger of the gods" of Roman mythology.

8. This top selling General motors marque launched its first watch collection in 2007. The watch collection pays tribute to co-founder of the brand, who was born in a family of a watchmaker and in his childhood helped his father at the workbench. Identify the marque.

9. This French automobile manufacturer shocked the world in 1934 with the innovative Traction Avant, the world's first mass-production front wheel drive car. Its significant models include HY, The Duck, Goddess and CX. Being a keen marketer, it used Eiffel tower as the world's largest advertising sign as recorded in the Guinness Book of Records. Identify the automobile manufacturer.

10. Which Swedish car manufacturer is the exclusive automobile royal warrant holder as appointed by H.M., the King of Sweden?

Ashok Kumar, Anoop Kumar, and Kishore Kumar raced with Chevrolet cars in the movie 'Chalti Ka Naam Gaadi'.

11. The emblem of this company has evolved from the circular Rapp Motorenwerke company logo. The Rapp logo was combined with colors of the flag of Bavaria to produce the logo so familiar today. Identify the German automobile manufacturer.

12. Which British manufacturer of sports and racing cars based at Hethel, Norfolk and founded by F1 legend Cloin Chapman had drivers like Ayrton Senna, Graham Hill and Stirling Moss in its racing division?

13. This German car corporation owns major stakes in aerospace group EADS, McLaren Group, Japanese truck maker Mitsubishi Fuso Truck and Bus Corporation. Identify the auto major.

14. 'The Whitbread Round the World Race' is a yacht race around the world, held every three years. Who is the current owner of it?

15. Name the car company that used to market itself as a 'different kind of car company'. It owes it origin to a revolutionary new, small-car project started in June, 1982 by Alex C. Mair.

16. With which automobile brand would you associate 'The Spirit of Ecstacy' or 'The Flying Lady'?

17. It was launched in a converted factory in 1903 with $28,000 in

cash from twelve investors, most notably John and Horace Dodge (who would later eatablish their own car company). The company owns a one-third controlling interest in Mazda of Japan and a small holding in former subsidiary Aston Martin of England. Identify the American multinational.

18. Which company was formed from the remnants of the Henry Ford Company when Henry Ford departed along with several of his key partners?

19. It is an Italian manufacturer of racing cars and sports cars and its emblem is a trident. Its current models include Quattroporte and GranTurismo. Which car maker?

20. Which company's line of luxury cars is branded 'Acura' in North America and China?

Answers

1. Audi company; the Audi emblem is four overlapping rings that represent the four marques of Auto Union. It symbolizes the amalgamation of Audi with DKW, Horch and Wanderer: the first ring represents Audi, the second represents DKW, third is Horch, and the fourth and last ring Wanderer.

2. Bentley Motors Limited; founded in England in 1919 by Walter Owen Bentley, known as W.O. Bentley or just "W.O". Since 1998 the company has been owned by the Volkswagen Group of Germany.

3. Volkswagen-Beetle

4. General Motors

5. Volkswagen-Beetle

6. Volvo

7. Mercury

8. Chevrolet; the watch collection pays tribute to Louis Chevrolet, co-founder of the brand, who was born in a family of a watchmaker and in his childhood helped his father at the workbench. The collection was called 'Frontenac', the name inherited from the race car company founded by Louis Chevrolet.

9. Citroën

10. Saab Automobile AB

11. BMW (English: Bavarian Motor Works)

12. Lotus

13. Daimler AG

14. Volvo

15. Saturn

16. Rolls Royce

17. Ford Motor Company

18. Cadillac

19. Maserati

20. Honda Motor Company

✠✠✠

Auto Expo II

Questions

1 Which brand's name, latin for 'I roll', was thought to be a good trademark for a ball bearing as well as for an automobile?

2 Name the company that was founded by a race car driver and William Durant in 1911 and is famous for its 'Bowtie emblem' logo.

3 Drums is a subsidiary of which company? They are in the business of manufacturing acoustic and electronic drum kits, as well as other percussion instruments, marching band equipment, and drum hardware and say '100% handcrafted'.

4 The logo of this company is said to be symbolic of two people (the company and customer) shaking hands. Company's name means modernity in Korean. The company's first model, the 'Cortina', was released in cooperation with Ford Motor Company in 1968. Identify the company.

5 Name the Japanese car, commercial vehicle and heavy truck manufacturing company that takes its name from a river and means 'fifty bells' in English.

Maruti donated the first Maruti 800 produced by it to The Lord Venkateshwara Temple at Tirupati.

6. The company was founded as the Swallow Sidecar Company in Blackpool in 1922 by two motorcycle enthusiasts, William Lyons and William Walmsley, changing to SS Cars Ltd in 1934. The company bought the Daimler Motor Company in 1960 from Birmingham Small Arms Company (BSA). The Ford Motor Company purchased the company in September 1989 and sold it in 2008. Identify the luxury car manufacturer.

7. This German company's first car was named as 'Dixi', the company's original slogan was 'Freude am Fahren' which translates to 'Joy in Driving'. Identify the company.

8. This company started out as a tractor building company in the Italian village of Sant'Agata Bolognese. However, founder's priorities changed when he went to meet Enzo Ferrari at the Ferrari factory to complain about the quality of the clutch in his Ferrari 250, and received a dismissive answer from Ferrari, who suggested he should look after his tractors. This incident led to the foundation of which auto major?

9. Who opened the trade session at the NYSE on 14 February 2002?

10. The first prototype 'centre steer' of this automobile company was built on a Jeep chassis. A distinctive feature is their bodies, constructed of a lightweight rustproof proprietary alloy of aluminium and magnesium called Birmabright. This material was used owing to post war steel shortages and a plentiful supply of post-war aircraft aluminium. Identify this automobile company.

11. Rafael Nadal is the global brand ambassador for this Korean carmaker. Its name is roughly translated as 'arise or come up out of Asia or rising out of Asia'. Identify this Korean carmaker.

At the beginning, Opel just produced sewing machines in a cowshed in Rüsselsheim.

12. In 1983, Eiji Toyoda summoned a secret meeting of company executives, to whom he posed the question, "Can we create a luxury vehicle to challenge the world's best?" This question prompted the company to embark on a top-secret project, codenamed F1 ("Flagship" and "No. 1 vehicle"). The name has been attributed to the combination of the words – luxury and elegance, while another theory claims it is an acronym for "luxury exports to the U.S." Identify the automaker and the brand.

13. This is a German luxury car manufacturer founded in 1909 by Wilhelm with his son Karl as director. The company was originally a subsidiary of Luftschiffbau Zeppelin GmbH and was itself known as 'Luftfahrzeug-Motoreinbau GmbH' (literally 'Airship Engine Company') until 1918. Identify the luxury car manufacturer owned by Daimler AG.

14. Name the Hiroshima headquartered automotive manufacturer whose name coincides with the anglicised pronunciation of the founder's name, Jujiro Matsuda, who was interested in spirituality, and chose to rename the firm in honour of both his family and Zoroastrianism.

15. Name the car company that used an American Indian headdress as a logo until 1956 that was replaced by an American Indian red arrowhead design in 1957. The name of the brand is derived from

an American Indian chief who led an unsuccessful uprising against the British shortly after the French and Indian War.

16. Originally named Alex Wilson and Company, much of this brand's success during the early years is given to a man called Laurence Pomeroy. It is named after the residential area in which it was formed. Most current models of this brand are right-hand drive derivatives of GM's Opel brand. Which automobile brand?

17. This advertising icon was created by a French cartoonist Marius Rossillon, popularly known as O'Galop, who showed the founder of the company a rejected image he had created for Munich brewery—a large, regal figure holding a huge glass of beer and quoting Horace's phrase that meant literally "Now it is to be drunk" in Latin. The founder suggested replacing the man with a figure made from the company's main product and the icon was born. Identify the icon.

The original trademark brand name application for Jeep was filed in February 1943 by Willys-Overland.

18. Which auto brand is said to get its name from the Slavic goddess of love, beauty and domestic harmony?

19. In automobile history, the phrase 'Fix it again, Tony' was popular mocking of a famous brand in its early years during its launch in the US. Name the brand.

20. In Dan Brown's novel Angels & Demons, the members of the Swiss Guard drive this company's sedans. It has been a part of the Fiat Group since 1986. It was founded as Società Anonima Italiana Darracq (SAID) in 1906 by the French automobile firm of Alexandre Darracq, with some Italian investors. Identify this brand mentioned in Angels & Demons.

Answers

1. Volvo
2. Chevrolet
3. Yamaha Corporation
4. Hyundai Motor Company
5. Isuzu Motors Ltd.
6. Jaguar
7. BMW
8. Lamborghini
9. Honda manufactured humanoid robot (ASIMO)
10. Land Rover
11. Kia Motors
12. Toyota and Lexus
13. Maybach
14. Mazda
15. Pontiac
16. Vauxhall Motors
17. Bibendum
18. Lada
19. FIAT; **F**ix **i**t **a**gain, **T**ony
20. Alfa Romeo

✠✠✠

Back to B - School

Questions

1. Which term was coined by the famous marketing strategist Jerry Welsh, while he was working as the manager of global marketing efforts for the American Express Company in the 1980s?

2. Which framework was introduced by Steiner and Andrews for analyzing an organisation's external environment from various angles?

3. It broke all records for being the most reprinted in the annals of the publication. Which paper?

4. What did Albert Humphrey develop while heading a research project at Stanford University in the 1960s and 1970s using data from Fortune 500 companies?

5. What is the name of an unconventional way of performing promotional activities on a very low budget, as described by Jay Conrad Levinson in this popular 1984 book?

    Yoyodyne was the first Internet-based direct marketer, founded by Seth Godin, and acquired by Yahoo! in 1998.

6. I am the co-owner of Stacey's Cafe in downtown Pleasanton, California. And I'm the owner and ironically incompetent active manager for Stacey's in Dublin, California. Who am I?

7. Name the matrix that was created by Bruce Henderson in 1970 to help corporations with analyzing their business units or product lines and allocate resources.

8. Which term was first published in 1969 by Jack Trout in the publication Industrial Marketing and defined as a game people play in today's me-too market place?

9.   Which term was coined by globalization guru, Goerge Yip to describe a firm's response to a competitive attack in one country by retaliation in another?

10. Which framework was developed by Michael Porter for analyzing the various activities a firm performs in order to create value for its customers?

E. Jerome McCarthy - an American marketing professor at Michigan State University is known for his concept of 4Ps of marketing.

11. Which modern marketing terminology owes its origin to how owners of different cattle were recognized from one another?

12. When he was 19, he was recruited by the manager of the local Union Carbide battery plant. He worked there for four years. He was the co-founder and became CEO of Praja Inc . The company eventually laid off 1/3rd of its workforce and was sold to TIBCO. Identify him.

13. | List I | List II |
     | --- | --- |
     | Television / Home cinema | 1. Movie theaters |
     | Steamships | 2. Sailing ships |
     | Automobiles | 3. Rail transport |
     | Minicomputers | 4. Mainframes |
     | Missile weapons | 5. Artillery |

     What does this list indicate?

14. Which 1968 publication had sold 1.2 million reprints by 1987 and was the most requested article from the Harvard Business Review?

15. It is also known as Finagle's law or Sod's law. It is named after a test engineer for the McDonnell Douglas aerospace manufacturer during a series of G-force experiments carried out in 1949 by the US air force to assess the tolerance of the human body to acceleration. Which law?

16. He was the first to propose that a surgical nurse serve as "caddy" to a surgeon, by handing surgical instruments to the surgeon as called for. He also devised the standard techniques used by armies around the world to teach recruits how to rapidly disassemble and reassemble their weapons even when blindfolded or in total darkness. Identify him.

17. Who is the author of a popular 1984 book "Guerrilla marketing" ?

18. The tradition of this often dates back to centuries and they differ from country to country. In France they have the Diplome Grand Ecole, in Germany the Diplom Kaufmann/ Frau, in Italy it's the Laurea Magistrale. How is it commonly know it in India?

19. The term has been very much in the news. It refers to the ownership interest acquired by a company's executives on favourable terms, to reflect the value they have added and will continue to add to the company. What is this two word term?

20. Born in Vienna, I moved to USA in 1937. I was awarded the Presidential Medal of Freedom by George W Bush in 2002. Recently, I founded leader-to-leader foundation. My most controversial work is on compensation schemes in which I said that senior management should not be compensated more than 20 times the lowest paid employee. Who am I?

Answers

1. Ambush Marketing
2. PEST Analysis
3. Marketing Myopia by Theodore Levitt
4. SWOT Analysis
5. Guerilla Marketing
6. Scott Adams
7. BCG matrix
8. Positioning
9. Counterparry
10. Value Chain
11. Brand
12. C K Prahlad
13. Disruptive Innovations
14. "One More Time, How Do You Motivate Employees?" by Maslow.
15. Murphy's Law; Murphy's law is an adage that is typically stated as: "Anything that can go wrong, will go wrong".
16. Frank Bunker Gilbreth, Sr
17. Jay Conrad Levinson
18. MBA
19. Sweat Equity
20. Peter Drucker

✠✠✠

Banking Conclave

Questions

1. Who began his financial career with the stock broking firm Harkisandass Lukhmidass and subsequently joined ICICI and was its chairman until his retirement in 1972?

2. Name the bank that became the first bank in the world to offer an overdraft facility in 1728.

3. This bank owes its origins to the business communities of the China coast in the 1860s. At that time, the finance of trade in the region was not well developed and most transactions were still handled by the European trading houses, or hongs, rather than by professional banks. By the early 1860s, local businessmen needed larger and more sophisticated facilities. The founding of the bank by Thomas Sutherland in 1865 answered this need. Identify the bank.

4. Which bank was founded by the family of Devkaran Nanjee under the name Devkaran Nanjee Banking Company Ltd?

5. The Capital and Counties Bank, founded in 1834, had 473 branches when it merged with Lloyds Bank Ltd in 1918. Name the author who was a customer of a branch of the bank located at Oxford Street and also mentions the branch as a banker to the central character of his books.

> *Banca Monte dei Paschi di Siena S.p.A. (MPS) is the oldest surviving bank in the world. Founded in 1472 by the Magistrate of the city state of Siena, Italy, as a mount of piety, it has been operating ever since.*

6. The sculptures of Yaksha and Yakshini flank the entrance of the New Delhi Office of the Reserve Bank of India. The sculptures were executed by which Indian artist?

7. Name the bank that was founded in 1906 in the Temple Town of Udupi, by a small group of philanthropists led by Khan Bahadur Haji Abdulla Haji Kasim Saheb Bahadur because of the absence of such a facility in Udupi.

8. He describes the Depository Bank of Zurich as a twenty-four hour Geldschrank bank at 24 Rue Haxo in Paris, offering the full modern array of anonymous services in the tradition of the Swiss numbered account. Who is he?

9. What was established on 1 April 1935 on the recommendations of the Hilton Young Commission?

10. Name the bank that was registered on 11 November 1919 as a limited company in Mumbai and was inaugurated by Mahatma Gandhi.

11. Which bank is also known as the "Queen's Bank" to many by virtue of it being reputed to be the bankers to the British Royal Family and an ATM of the bank is in the basement of Buckingham Palace for use by the Royal Family and Household?

12. The idea of which bank with Indian capital and management was conceived by Ghanshyam Das Birla during the Quit India movement of 1942?

Famed novelist and philosopher Ayn Rand was a close associate of Alan Greenspan who served as the Chairman of the Federal Reserve Bank of the United States from 1987 to 2006.

13. Which bank was founded by Annamalai and Ramaswami Chettiar in 1907 in response to the financial crash faced by two leading trading companies in Madras, Arbuthnot's and Binny's?

14. Which bank's logo was designed by Anton Stankowski and intended to represent growth within a risk-controlled framework in 1972?

15. Which Indian bank carries an image of a dog in its logo?

16. The central bank of which country is sometimes known by the metonym-The Old Lady of Threadneedle Street?

17. Name the RBI governor who oversaw the post-partition division of the assets and liabilities of the Reserve Bank between India and Pakistan when British India was partitioned into India and Pakistan in 1947.

18. Name the business group that is the promoter of IndusInd Bank in India.

19. Van Gogh Preferred Banking was introduced in India by this bank in the year 2002. Offered across all 31 branches in 23 cities, it has emerged as the preferred choice for clients for both wealth management and business banking requirements. Identify the bank.

20. Which bank helped underwrite the initial public offering of The Coca-Cola Company in 1919?

Answers

1. Hasmukhbhai Parekh
2. Royal Bank of Scotland
3. HSBC
4. Dena Bank
5. Sir Arthur Conan Doyle
6. Ramkinkar Baij
7. Corporation Bank
8. Dan Brown
9. RBI
10. Union Bank of India
11. Coutts
12. United Commercial Bank (UCO Bank)
13. Indian Bank
14. Deutsche Bank
15. Syndicate Bank
16. United Kingdom
17. C. D. Deshmukh
18. Hinduja
19. ABN AMRO (now RBS)
20. Sun Trust Bank

✠✠✠

Big Bosses

Questions

1. He served as the Chairman of SEBI's 17-Member Committee on Corporate Governance constituted in mid-1999, and as Chairman of SEBI's Committee on Insider Trading and his Report on Corporate Governance became the cornerstone of Corporate Governance practices in India. Who is he?

2. Companies today are increasingly recognising human capital as a form of wealth. "Our core corporate assets walk out every evening, mentally and physically tired." So said one of the most sought-after CEOs of India Inc. to a graduating class of Wharton. Name the CEO.

3. What is the significance of the phrase "I Am Chairman Of Chrysler Corporation Always"?

Apple lured John Sculley away from Pepsi because they wanted him to apply his marketing skills to the personal computer market. Steve Jobs successfully sealed the deal with his legendary pitch to Sculley, asking him whether he preferred to "sell sugar water for the rest of your life or come with me and change the world?"

4. The founder of this company was a star employee of IBM who finished his year's sales quota in a record 2 months and also saved two of his employees who were taken hostage by the Iranian Government just before the revolution in 1979. This incident was later turned into a bestselling novel 'On Wings of Eagle' by Ken Follett. Identify the founder and the company.

5. He was born as Andras Grof and as the Nazis swept to power in Europe his name was changed to Andras Malesevics because they were Jewish family. When he came to the United States, what name did he finally assume?

6. Name the CEO whose life was turned into a comic book series in Japan in 2002 and later published as a separate book.

7. This company was founded in 1951 in San Diego and is listed on the NYSE. It has a fictional CEO. Name him and the company.

8. The first non-American CEO of this company, who died recently, once said he would not let the organisation get "fat, dumb and happy." His personal motto was 'Life is not a rehearsal.' Who are we referring to?

9. This Salomon Brothers' Chairman and CEO was called 'The King of Wall Street' by BusinessWeek in 1987. But, he was forced to resign in 1991 when a company trader was found to have violated Treasury auction rules. Warren Buffett took over Salomon's reins from him. Who is being referred to here?

10. This company traces its origins to 1984, when the founder created PCs Limited while a student at the University of Texas at Austin. Identify the famous CEO of this Fortune 500 company.

Ursula Burns is the first Afro-American woman CEO to head a Fortune 500 company – XEROX.

11. Which company and its CEO inspired Ashutosh Gowariker to make the Hindi movie Swades with Shah Rukh Khan in the lead role?

12. This famous CEO was a radio operator with Marconi Wireless Telegraph company when he picked up distress signals from the RMS Titanic after it hit an iceberg on 14 April 1912. Name the person and the company of which he became an integral part.

13. Name the managing director of a large business group who studied to be a filmmaker before he graduated from Harvard Business School. He has produced a short film on the Kumbh Mela and his business group is currently planning a foray into the media and entertainment sector.

Paul Allen, co-founder of Microsoft, is the owner and executive producer of Vulcan Productions, a filmmaking company headquartered in Seattle.

14. At this company, workers choose their bosses. Everyone gets to know the company's financial position. Nearly a third of the employees determine their own salaries. The President of this company who has been instrumental in bringing these path-breaking initiatives was able to make the company grow by a whopping 900 per cent in 10 years. Can you name the Brazilian company and its famous President?

15. This famous CEO was inspired by the paper written by Edgar F. Codd on relational database systems called "A Relational Model of Data for Large Shared Data Banks" and founded Software Development Laboratories (SDL) in 1977 which is known by another name today. Identify the CEO.

16. In 1991, he co-founded Ink Development, a pen-based computing start-up that was later rebranded as an e-commerce company. He was only 28 when he sat down over a long holiday weekend to write the original computer code for what eventually became an Internet superbrand. Who are we talking about?

17. Born in the family's sod house in White, South Dakota, his business sense and emphasis on research and development helped bring 3M back from the brink of bankruptcy and turn it into the large, multinational corporation. Who is he?

18. He was an American business executive, public administrator, and the author of pioneering work in management theory and organizational studies. He worked for AT&T for about 40 years. His landmark 1938 book, Functions of the Executive, sets out a theory of organization and of the functions of executives in organizations. Who is he?

23 and Me is a privately held personal genomics and biotechnology company co-founded by Anne Wojcicki who is married to Google co-founder Sergey Brin.

19. In the 1990s, he submitted so many high scores for the game Tetris to Nintendo Power that they would no longer print his scores, so he started sending them in under the name "Evets Kainzow". He founded a new venture called CL 9, which developed and brought the first universal TV remote control to market in 1987. In 2001, he co-founded Wheels of Zeus to create wireless GPS technology to "help everyday people find everyday things." He competed on Season 8 of Dancing With The Stars in 2009 where he danced with Karina Smirnoff. Who is he?

20. Name the co-founder of a internet company who is an active investor in alternative energy companies, such as Tesla Motors, which developed the Tesla Roadster, a 220-mile (350 km) range battery electric vehicle.

Answers

1. Kumar Mangalam Birla
2. NR Narayan Murthy
3. To enable the employees of Chrysler Corporation remember the spelling of Lee Iacocca.
4. Ross Perot and EDS
5. Andrew Grove; the former Intel boss
6. Carlos Ghosn, CEO of Renault and Nissan
7. Jack; the fictional CEO of Jack In The Box, a fast food company.
8. Charlie Bell; the former CEO of McDonald's
9. John Gutfreund
10. Michael Dell
11. Vikram Akula, CEO of SKS Microfinance
12. David Sarnoff, RCA Corporation
13. Anand Mahindra of the Mahindra & Mahindra Group.
14. Semco, Ricardo Semler
15. Larry Ellison
16. Pierre Omidyar
17. William L. Mcknight
18. Chester Irving Barnard
19. Steve Woznaik; "Woz" is an acronym for Wheels of Zeus. Reversing "Evets Kainzow" gives Steve Woznaik.
20. Larry Page

✠✠✠

Brand Logos

Questions

1. 2008 saw the release of a revised version of the 2005 logo of this automobile brand. Through the new-look Griffin pays homage to this brand's 100 year-plus manufacturing heritage in the UK. Identify the automobile brand.

2. The star in which brand's logo comes from a tattoo that the founder got as a teenager when he worked on a Nantucket whaling ship?

3. Some of the company's original logos include an elephant (after which some of its lagers are named) and the swastika. Use of the latter was discontinued in the 1930s because of its association with political parties in neighboring Germany. Identify the company.

4. This brand's logo is an image of a "twin-tailed siren". At the beginning of September 2006 and then again in early 2008, it temporarily reintroduced its original brown logo on paper hot drink cups to show the company's heritage from the Pacific Northwest and to celebrate 35 years of business. Which brand?

Buick's emblem consists of three shields, each bisected diagonally to the right by a straight line, the shields arranged touching each other in a left-diagonal pattern, inside a circle. This design, known as the Trishield, was adopted in 1959 for the 1960 models and represents the three models that comprised the lineup that year—LeSabre, Invicta, and Electra.

5. Which German manufacturer of writing instruments, watches and accessories, often is identified by their famous "White Star" logo that is also referred to as an edelweiss?

6. The old factory of this brand remained empty until around 2003 when it was converted to a industrial park called Arrow Park. The founder of the company received a patent on his "Lucky Curve" feed in 1894 and created Quink "quick drying ink" in 1931. Identify the brand.

7. The original logo and product labels of which company were designed by an art student, Jeff Harris, who was paid £20?

8. Which artist in 1969 designed the logo of Chupa Chups – a Spanish lollipop company?

9. Which company's logo is said to be a modified version of the Cross of Lorraine?

In 1945, Fortune magazine named Betty Crocker, mascot of General Mills, the second most popular American woman just behind Eleanor Roosevelt.

10. When Francesco Baracca died in WWI, his mother asked her industrialist friend to immortalize her son in a certain way. He chose his company's logo as a tribute to Baracca's plane. Which company?

11. It was created by an illustrator named Tom Browne to be a likeness of John Walker in traditional attire. In the logo, the man is walking forward, which Diageo says symbolizes forward thinking and the pursuit for excellence. How do we popularly know the logo?

12. The logo colours signify:

    Red Square – Leadership, passion

    White Swirl – Purity of purpose, invigorating properties of coffee

    Green Stroke – 125 years of coffee growing heritage of this vertically integrated group. The font used for "Café" is called SLURRY. The font looks as though the letters have congealed out of a liquid. Which company's logo has been described?

The previous logo of 'The English Premier League' showed a blue lion wearing a crown with its right foot over a football. On 12 February 2007, it was modified slightly to show the lion facing the viewer and the ball under the left foot instead of the right.

13. The names of these mascots came from an earlier radio ad for the same product, which went as follows:

    "Listen to the fairy song of health, the merry chorus sung by _____ ,_____ ,_____ as they merrily ____, ____, and ___ in a bowl of milk. If you've never heard food talking, now is your chance."

    The last three blanks gave their name to the mascots. Which mascots?

14. The logo of the company is representative of a light that has three crossed tuning forks. Which company?

15. Identify the European automobile manufacturer whose logo shows a lion rearing up on its hind legs, to adopt the posture of the lion on the coat of arms of Franche-Comté, birthplace of its business. Which company's logo?

16. The initial logo of this brand started by Allen Lane was created by the then twenty-one-year-old office junior Edward Young. The color schemes included: orange and white for general fiction, green and white for crime fiction, red and white for travel and adventure, blue and white for biographies; and the rarer purple and white for essays and belles letters and grey and white for world affairs. Which company's logo was designed by Edward Young?

17. Which company's logo depicts nine small pyramids, which combine into a single larger pyramid?

The three dots in the Domino's Pizza logo represent the first three stores of DPZ that had opened. The company logo was originally planned to add a new dot with the addition of every new store, but this idea quickly faded as Domino's experienced rapid growth.

18. This logo was designed by a graphic design student in 1971. A faculty member asked the student to help him with some work for his new sportswear company. Of the various choices, the teacher picked one, saying: "I don't love it, but it'll grow on me." Which logo?

19. Which corporate logo was designed by George Dexter?

20. Slats, born in Dublin Zoo on 20 March 1919, was the first lion used as the mascot and logo of this company. He was trained by Volney Phifer to growl rather than roar and, for the next couple of years, the lion toured with this company's promoters to market it. Which company?

Answers

1. Vauxhall Motors
2. Macy's
3. Carlsberg
4. Starbucks
5. Montblanc International Gmbh
6. Parker Pen Company
7. Bodyshop
8. Salvador Dali
9. Exxon
10. Ferrari; the industrialist friend was Enzo Ferrari, and the logo was the prancing horse.
11. Striding Man Logo
12. Café Coffee Day
13. Snap, Crackle And Pop – The mascots of Kellogg's Rice Krispies.
14. Yamaha
15. Peugeot
16. Penguin Books
17. DLF
18. Swoosh, of Nike
19. The Golden Arches of McDonald's
20. MGM; the mascot was called Leo the Lion. After Slats' death, four other lions have been used as Leo the Lion.

✠ ✠ ✠

Book Fair

Questions

1. Who is the author of the book 'Talking Straight'? It was written to balance Akio Morita's 'Made in Japan', a non-fiction book praising Japan's postwar hardworking culture. 'Talking Straight' praised the innovation and creativity of the Americans.

2. This book begins with the words "Business is going to change more in the next ten years than it has in the last fifty" and ends with "I strongly believe that if companies empower their employees to solve problems and give them potent tools to do this with, they will always be amazed at how much creativity and initiative will blossom forth." Name the book.

The modern mass market paperback books were first produced by Albatross Books – a German publishing house.

3. Who is the author of the books – 'The Five-Day Course in Thinking', 'The Mechanism of the Mind' and 'Six Action Shoes'?

4. The book 'The Man Who Owns the News' is about which famous business personality?

5. This metaphor was coined by the economist Adam Smith in his book 'The Wealth of Nations'. He demonstrated that, in a free market, an individual pursuing his own self-interest tends to also promote the good of his community as a whole through a principle. Identify the metaphor.

6. 'Anatomy of Greed' is a book by Brian Cruver and released by Avalon Publishing in the United States and by Random House in Europe. In 2003, CBS aired a television movie based on Cruver's book entitled The Crooked E. This book is an author's perspective as an employee who worked for the energy giant on which the book is based. Which energy giant?

7. Whose autobiography is titled 'Pizza Tiger'?

8. The bestseller book 'The Rogue Trader' is whose own account of his role in the ruin of Barings bank?

9. Who is the furniture dealer being referred to in the book titled 'A Testament of a Furniture Dealer'?

10. 'Quality and Me: Lessons from an Evolving Life' is an autobiography of which quality guru? He argued in one of his books that "doing it right the first time" is less expensive than the costs of detecting and correcting nonconformities.

11. 'The Triumph of the American Imagination' is a book written by Neal Gabler about which synergistic empire?

12. 'The Japan That Can Say No' refers to the authors' vision of a Japanese Government that is more than a mere "yes man" to the United States. Name the more famous author of the essay.

13. 'Grinding it Out' is the autobiography of which famous entrepreneur?

14. This book by John C Tarrant, subtitled 'The Man Who Invented the Corporate Society' is about a writer, management consultant, and self-described social ecologist. Identify this management consultant who invented the corporate society.

In 1475, Englishman William Caxton produced the first book printed in English, The Recuyell of the Historyes of Troye.

15. Following is an excerpt from the author's note of a book:

   'A' is what 'X' advised the graduating class of Stanford University in his commencement address to the class of 2005. And that is the motto by which all the entrepreneurs I have met for this book have lived.

   Identify A and X.

16. 'Nuts – Crazy Recipe for Business and Personal Success' by Keven and Jackie Freiberg is a book about a company that was started when Rollin King described the concept to Kelleher over dinner by drawing on a paper napkin a triangle symbolizing the routes. The company's stock ticker symbol is LUV and its advertising slogans include "Just Plane Smart," "The Somebody Else Up There Who Loves You" with the current one being "A Symbol of Freedom". About which company has the book been written?

17. Which company was founded in 1935 by Sir Allen Lane and is owned by Pearson PLC?

18. 'Pour Your Heart Into It' is a book that traces the growth and development of a company from a single store in Seattle to the international business it has become today. One of the initial goals of the founder was to provide people with a "third place" to gather. Name the company.

19. A book by Sara Gay Forden, subtitled 'Sensational story of Murder, Madness, Glamour and Greed' is the story of which fashion house?

20. Identify the author of the book 'Free Prize Inside: The Next Big Marketing Idea'.

Answers

1. Lee Iacocca
2. Business @ the Speed of Thought
3. Edward de Bono
4. Rupert Murdoch
5. Invisible Hand
6. Enron
7. Tom Monaghan; Thomas Stephen, "Tom" Monaghan is an entrepreneur and activist who founded Domino's Pizza in 1960. He owned the Detroit Tigers from 1983-1992.
8. Nick Leeson
9. Ingvar Kamprad; Ingvar Feodor Kamprad is a Swedish business magnate and the founder of IKEA, a retail (specialty) company.
10. Phil Crosby
11. Disney
12. Akio Morita
13. Ray Kroc; Raymond Albert "Ray" Kroc was an American businessman who took over the small-scale McDonald's Corporation franchise in 1954 and built it into the most successful fast food operation in the world. He was a multi-mixer milkshake machine salesman before taking the franchise of McDonald's Corporation and therefore, the name of the autobiography.
14. Peter Drucker
15. A – Stay Hungry Stay Foolish ; X – Steve Jobs
16. Southwest Airlines
17. Penguin Books
18. Starbucks
19. Gucci
20. Seth Godin

✠ ✠ ✠

Brand India

Questions

1. The full form of the brand means 'the Shop of the Magnanimous' in Punjabi. It has been involved in several charitable and social activities through its sister orgnaization, Mahashay Chuni Lal Charitable Trust. Name the brand.

2. Started by Balkrishan Goenka with a polyester yarn facility in 1985, the insignia of this company is a creative visualization of a flying pair of sea gulls. Identify the company.

3. The history of this company dates back to 1924 when the Maiyya family started a small restaurant in Bangalore. In 1951, the restaurant came to be known as Mavilli Tiffin Room. How is this company better known?

4. This company was founded in 1979 by a Delhi-based entrepreneur who named his company after his neighbour's dog. He started out by selling song books, posters and leather patches, before hitting big with another product. Which company?

5. Vadilal Shah, while working with his father in their family shop specialising in spices and dry fruits observed keenly the diligence with which housewives bought various spices from his shop to blend in their kitchen. The observations led to the development of which brand?

The acclaimed film maker Satyajit Ray designed the Rupa logo and all he asked for in return were some books!

6. Which company founded by Rajesh Kumar Drolia was originally incorporated as Creative Stationery Products Pvt. Ltd.?

7. The company was run by the Arya brothers: Naveen, Anil and Bimal. These brothers spotted a huge opportunity in the mosquito repellent business way back in 1990. They collaborated with a Japanese company known as Earth Chemical Company. Identify the company started by the three brothers and their most famous brand.

8. Odhavji Raghavji Patel, the founder of the world's biggest wall clock manufacturing company, established Ajanta Transistor Clock Manufacturing Company in 1970 in Gujarat. What is the name of his second most popular brand which they use for other electronic products like calculators, phones and time pieces?

9. Identify this Indian brand that was created in the 1940s by P L Lamba to cater to American soldiers who were stationed in Delhi during World War II. The founder used to dish the brand out from a hand-held wooden machine.

10. Girish Patel diversified into the FMCG sector in 1987 with a solitary product, Moov, after the OTC business that his father ran started showing signs of fatigue. Today, the company that started with Rs 57 lakh capital has 15 products in its portfolio. Identify the company.

11. Which company was started in 1959 by an entrepreneur H.D. Vasudeva, in technical collaboration with a British company?

The brand LGAsafoetida manufactured by Laljee Godhoo & Comapny is almost 110 years old and has never indulged in any marketing practice since its inception.

12. The inception of which group took place way back in mid seventies when two childhood friends, Mr. R.S. Agarwal and Mr. R.S. Goenka left their high profile jobs with the Birla Group to set up Kemco Chemicals, an Ayurvedic medicine and cosmetic manufacturing unit in Kolkata in 1974?

13. Which company started operations with Horse Brand Ink Powders and Tablets in 1933?

14. Rajesh Batra, a former national tennis champion, and his brother Rajiv Batra started a sportswear company because they could not find good quality T shirts. By what name is this company known?

15. This brand's image is the brainchild of the founder's son, Murari Mohan Dutta. On 15 August 1947, Calcutta news papers carried an advertisement informing audiences that from two specified city outlets, it would be distributed free to anyone who asks for it during the day. Which brand?

16. Founder M.P. Ramachandran started the company in 1984 from Kerala with one brand – a liquid fabric whitener. It was launched nationally in 1997 and the size of the brand then was Rs 150 crore. Identify the company and the brand.

17. Which company owes its origin to a distribution business of speciality chemicals manufactured by a German company by BK Parekh? The name of the most famous brand of this company comes from 'Federal Dyes'.

18. What was established as a patent medicine business at Bombay in 1893 by K. Nageswara Rao Pantulu who was a journalist, social reformer and freedom fighter?

19. Which brand was originally a vision of Tribhuvandas Kishibhai Patel?

20. This detergent brand started as an after-office business in 1969—the founder would bicycle through Ahmedabad selling handmade packets from door to door at one third the price of leading detergents. He later set up a shop and quickly grew enough to become India's largest selling detergent brand in the 1970s. Which detergent brand?

Answers

1. MDH (Mahashian Di Hatti)
2. Welspun Group
3. MTR foods (Mavilli Tiffin Room)
4. Archie's; the product was greeting cards
5. Everest Masala
6. Today's Writing Products Limited
7. Karamchand Appliances Pvt Ltd and Allout
8. Orpat (after his initials and surname)
9. Kwality Ice Cream
10. Paras Pharmaceuticals
11. Hawkins Cookers Limited
12. Emami
13. Camlin Limited
14. Proline
15. Boroline
16. Jyothy Laboratories and Ujala
17. Pidilite Industries; the product was Fevicol
18. Amrutanjan
19. Amul
20. Nirma

✠✠✠

Financial World

Questions

1. It's a technique that uses random variables to solve mathematical problems. Originally developed to build the atom bomb — under the Manhattan Project of the '40s — it is now used in the realm of finance also. It has a name of a city associated with it. Name this technique.

2. Who set up a company named Innovative Market Systems in 1981 using the severance package from his earlier employer – Solomon Brothers? Merrill Lynch became the new company's first customer in 1982.

3. Which financial giant was founded by two brothers – Henry and Emanuel and traces its origin to a dry-goods store opened in Alabama in 1844?

4. What term was coined by Deepak Mohoni in 1990, while writing market analysis columns for some of the business newspapers?

George Lane is a well known technical analyst. He coined the famous sentence: Trend is your friend

5. This business was set up in 1986 by Late S S Goenka, who was the founder of the company Peutronics Pvt. Ltd. His son Bharat was responsible for the development of the commercial software product which made a difficult subject very easy. Identify the software.

6. Which was the first company to publish an annual fiscal report in 1941? Its brokerage network is known as the "thundering herd".

7. President Franklin Roosevelt worked with Congress in the 1930's to pass a series of securities laws to help even the playing field in the markets. What agency was created to help enforce these laws?

8. What was established in Calcutta in 1818 by Bipin Behari Dasgupta and others? Europeans in India were its primary target market, and it charged Indians heftier premiums. It also funds close to 24.6% of the Indian Government's expenses.

9. It received its own Coat of Arms in 1923 and its motto is dictum meum pactum, "My word is my bond". Identify.

10. History of which company is the topic of the book "Three Cents A Week", referring to the premium paid by early policyholders? The company uses the Rock of Gibraltar as its logo.

Chris Gardner, whose autobiography was turned into the 2006 feature film The Pursuit of Happyness, interned at Dean Witter Reynolds.

IDENTIFY THE TERMS IN QUESTIONS 11-20.

11. A corporation without active business operations or significant assets.

12. The distortion that is caused in a company's financial statements due to accounting rules and regulations that must be followed.

13. A reference to auditors performing more careful due diligence when auditing companies, in order to prevent accounting errors.

14. A fraudulent accounting technique that involves a parent company making artificial paper-only transactions with its subsidiaries to hide losses the parent company has incurred through business activities.

15. When a regulated public utility business financially separates itself from a parent company that engages in non-regulated business.

16. The unethical practice of a broker trading an equity based on information from the analyst department before his or her clients have been given the information.

17. Legal barriers that prevent both the transference of inside information and the performance of financial transactions between commercial and investment banks.

18. A surge in the price of stocks that often occurs in the week between Christmas and New Year's Day.

19. A company set up in a tax haven and having no physical presence there other than a mailing address.

20. It is a defense strategy used against a hostile takeover. It is when a takeover target company launches a tender offer for the company that was trying to acquire it.

Answers

1. Monte Carlo Simulation
2. Michael Bloomberg
3. Lehman Brothers
4. Sensex
5. Tally
6. Merill Lynch
7. SEC (Securities and Exchange Commission)
8. LIC
9. London Stock Exchange
10. Prudential Insurance Company of America
11. Shell Corporation
12. Accounting Noise
13. Andersen Effect
14. Enronomics
15. Ringfencing
16. Front Running
17. Firewall
18. Santa Claus Rally
19. Letter-Box Company
20. Pac-Man Strategy

✠ ✠ ✠

Games People Play

Questions

1. This game's name is supposedly derived from the name of a Marsh, the location of the first recorded game. The game is played by two teams of seven and involves four balls. It is played on pitches that are typically in the shape of an oval, five hundred feet long and one hundred and eighty feet wide, with a small central circle of approximately two feet in diameter. Which game?

2. Which company's first toy hit was Mr. Potato Head, which the company purchased from inventor George Lerner in 1952?

3. Her full name is Barbara Millicent Roberts. She has been said to attend Willows High School and Manhattan International High School in New York City. She has an on-off romantic relationship with her beau Ken Carson. How is she popularly known?

4. Founded in 1932 by Ole Kirk Christiansen, this company's basic philosophy is that "good play" enriches a child's life and its subsequent adulthood. Which company?

Solitaire derives its name from a French word meaning 'Patience'.

5. What was created in 1987 as a result of joint venture between the world's largest toy manufacturer Hasbro and the Indian tyre major MRF?

6. In the 1960s, Geoffrey the Giraffe, an anthropomorphic cartoon giraffe, was introduced as its mascot. Identify the company.

7. Name the Japanese company that was founded by Marty Bromley (an American) to import pinball games to Japan for use on American military bases.

8. Arthur Wynne was a writer for the game page of the New York World at the turn of the 19th century. One winter afternoon in 1913, while trying to think up new types of games for the newspaper's special Christmas edition, he came up with an idea. The big break for

this came when two young Harvard graduates, Messrs Simon and Schuster, made a fortune in 1923 by leveraging on the idea. Identify the idea.

9.   Which company started with a toy shop called "Noah's Ark" in London in 1760? It opened its first store in Asia in Mumbai in 2010.

10. Identify the line of toys started by Hassenfeld Brothers in 1964, which they termed an "action figure" in order to market the toy to boys who wouldn't want to play with "dolls".

11. An architect and professor at the University of Budapest developed the first working prototype for these in 1974. He received a Hungarian patent in 1975. Professor created it as a teaching aid for his students to help them recognize three-dimensional spatial relationships. When he showed the working prototype to his students, it was an immediate hit. They are always made from virgin material and never use reground waste plastic. Identify.

Mr Potato Head was the first toy advertised on television and has remained in production since its debut.

12. Charles B Darrow in 1933 was given a license to print money. A couple of years later, the rights were purchased by someone else and they now print about $50 billion money every year. A total print run of more than three trillion dollars has been done by them. Who purchased the rights?

13. The game was played widely in ancient India by the name of Moksha Patamu. Moksha Patamu was perhaps invented by Hindu spiritual teachers to teach children about the effects of good deeds as opposed to bad deeds. It made its way to England, and was eventually introduced in the United States of America by game-pioneer Milton Bradley in 1943. Identify the game.

14. Identify the world's largest preschool products company founded by Herman, Irving and Helen whose first toy ever sold was "Dr. Doodle" in 1931.

15. Name the company that derives its name from the names of the founders – Elliot Handler and Harold Matson.

16. Which name was once used as a generic trademark for all die cast toy cars measuring approximately 2.5 inches (6.5 cm) in length, regardless of brand?

17. Which game originally appeared in 1896 is a simplification of the traditional Indian Cross and Circle game Pachisi and is called "Fia" in Sweden? It shares its name with an alternative rock band from St. Louis, Missouri.

18.   The inventor of this game – Alfred Butts originally called it 'Lexiko' and there was no board. That came later as the game changed its name to 'It' and then to 'Criss-Cross'. Butts made a few sets to sell to friends but it went unnoticed until 1948 when James Brunot thought it might have commercial possibilities. Which game?

19.   All of Mattel's preschool products are marketed under which brand name?

20.   This is a history based real time strategy game released in 1997, which was developed by Ensemble studios and published by Microsoft. In the first version of the game, the player is the leader of a historical tribe or civilization, and has to advance through four ages – stone age, tool age, bronze age and iron age. Identify the game.

Answers

1. Quidditch of Harry Potter fame
2. Hasbro
3. Barbie
4. Lego
5. Funskool
6. Toys "R" Us
7. Sega; it derives its name from Service Games of Japan.
8. Crossword
9. Hamleys
10. G.I. Joe
11. Rubik's cube
12. Parker Brothers that owns the rights for Monopoly game.
13. Snakes and Ladders
14. Fisher-Price
15. Mattel
16. Matchbox
17. Ludo
18. Scrabble
19. Fisher-Price
20. Age of Empires

✠✠✠

Geeks & Gizmos

Questions

1. Which company was founded in 1994, spurred by what its founder called "regret minimization framework", his effort to fend off regret for not staking a claim in the Internet gold rush?

2. What term was coined by Chris Anderson in an October 2004 *Wired* magazine article to describe the niche strategy of businesses, such as Amazon.com or Netflix, that sell a large number of unique items, each in relatively small quantities?

3. The first film to use this technology was A Clockwork Orange in 1971. Lisztomania in 1975 was the first film to use it in stereo and Batman Returns in 1992 was the first to use it in digital. What is it?

4. Which company can trace it roots back to 1930 when Dr. J. Clarence Karcher and Eugene McDermott founded Geophysical Service, a pioneering provider of seismic exploration services to the petroleum industry?

AOL began life as a short-lived venture called Control Video Corporation (or CVC), founded by Bill von Meister. Its sole product was an online service called GameLine for the Atari 2600 video game console after von Meister's idea of buying music on demand was rejected by Warner Brothers.

5. He was a Nobel Prize laureate in physics in 2000 for his invention of the integrated circuit in 1958 while working at Texas Instruments (TI). He is also the inventor of the handheld calculator and thermal printer. Who is he?

6. The current incarnation of which company is the result of a March 2000 merger between Confinity and X.com? Confinity was founded in December 1998 by Max Levchin, Peter Thiel, Luke Nosek, and Ken Howery, initially as a Palm Pilot payments and cryptography company.

7. Created by the Gretech Corporation of South Korea, its name means "bear" in Korean, and it uses a bear's paw as its symbol. Identify.

8. According to Earling, one of the first references to the term is by Garth Kidd in February, 1996. He described it as "a tendency to identify everything in the world as being made of four squares and attempt to determine 'where it fits in'". What effect?

9. This search engine was founded by Venky Harinarayan and Anand Rajaraman who were also the co-founders of Junglee, the first shopping search engine which was acquired by Amazon.com. Identify.

10. The format was originally created in 1986 by Phil Katz. The name meaning "speed" was suggested by Katz's friend, Robert Mahoney. They wanted to imply that their product would be faster than other formats of the time. Which format?

Steve Jobs was the official photographer in the wedding of Larry Ellison and Melanie Craft.

11. What was created by researchers at Digital Equipment Corporation's Western Research Laboratory who were trying to provide services to make finding files on the public network easier and is now owned by Yahoo!?

12. In the 1995 film Hackers, Dade Murphy correctly identifies my book, commenting that it is recognizable by "the nasty pink shirt the guy wears on the cover". Who am I?

13. What was originally developed by students at the École Centrale Paris as an academic project in 1996 and the icon used by it is a reference to the traffic cones collected by Ecole Centrale's Networking Students' Association?

14. He plays rhythm guitar in a Seattle band called Grown Men and is a part owner of the Seattle Sounders FC, a major league soccer franchise that began play in 2009. Identify him.

15. A chartered accountant based out of NCR-Delhi region, he is currently the C.E.O of his VC funded BPO company – Quattro. Identify him.

16. Gary Thuerk says people have one of three reactions when they meet him: "some are excited to meet someone with an unusual claim to fame; some want to beat him up on the spot; and others just avoid him like the plague." What is his unusual claim to fame?

IT mogul N. R. Narayan Murthy has modelled for Windows XP operating system.

17. Which company was founded in 2000 by Deep Kalra that had its beginnings in a small office in Okhla, New Delhi?

18. The idea for starting which company struck VSS Mani while doing a sales job with a yellow pages company called United Database India (UDI) in 1987?

19. He is the Chairman and Managing Director of People Group. He has also produced two movies by names Flavors & 99. Who is he?

20. Which company founded in July 2007 had one of its founders as Mark Pincus and its name comes from an English bulldog once owned by Mark Pincus?

Answers

1. Amazon
2. The Long Tail
3. Dolby
4. Texas Instruments
5. Jack St. Clair Kilby
6. Paypal
7. GOM player
8. Tetris
9. Kosmix
10. ZIP format
11. Alta Vista
12. Peter Norton
13. VLC player
14. Paul Allen
15. Raman Roy; he is known as the father of BPO revolution in India.
16. He is known for sending the first spam email
17. MakeMyTrip
18. Just Dial
19. Anupam Mittal (Shaadi.com)
20. Zynga

✠✠✠

Liquor and Liquer I

Questions

1. Which company has its origins in the Glasgow firm of Allan & Poynter, founded in November 1843 by John Poynter, a successful chemical manufacturer and William Allan, a ham curer? Their famous "double lion" symbol, recognisable the world over, remains the sign of the very best in blended Scotch whisky.

2. Introduced to Northern Europe by Dutch traders in the 16th Century, its name comes from the Dutch word meaning "burnt wine". For a time Leland Stanford, founder of Stanford University, was the world's largest producer of this. Identify.

3. It was founded in 1847 by the visionary brewer J.C. Jacobsen. In 1975, it introduced "Probably the best lager in the world" slogan with voice-over by Orson Welles. It was one of the major sponsors of Euro 2008.Which brand?

> *The world's highest distillery is the Kasauli distillery in the Himalaya mountains at an elevation of over 6,000 feet.*

4. This brand of whiskey was introduced by distiller Jack Daniel's nephew Lem Motlow after Jack's death in 1911 to symbolise mourning. It was expected to last a year but people liked it so much, it was never discontinued. Identify the brand.

5. Which brand can you associate with the advertising campaign "good things come to those who wait"?

6. What was created in 1908 by an illustrator named Tom Browne to be a likeness of the company's founder in traditional attire and is believed to symbolise forward thinking and the pursuit for excellence?

7. Which beer, now owned and marketed by Heineken, was founded in 1870 and named after the river on which the Dutch capital is situated? The river's water was used in the brewing as well as refrigeration.

8. Which scotch whisky was created when William Sanderson made up a hundred vattings and chose the one he and his friends liked best? It was recorded as Lewis Nixon's favorite liquor in the book and mini-series Band of Brothers.

9. This Puerto Rico headquartered family-owned spirits company's drinks are not found in Cuba today because the family members of this company initially supported the Cuban revolutionaries, including Fidel Castro and the broader M-26-7 movement. Identify this family-owned company.

10. It is the country cousin of Tequila. Its production and consumption is popularly associated with the Mexican state of Oaxaca. A number of objects are frequently added into its bottles like worms, scorpions, and decorative elements such as glass sculptures with gold leaf. What is it?

Glenfiddich means 'Valley of the deer' in Gaelic, hence the presence of a deer symbol on Glenfiddich bottles. Glenfiddich is the favourite drink of Inspector Morse, a fictional character in a series of thirteen detective novels by British author Colin Dexter.

11. Name the Scottish whiskey that is described in packaging and advertising as "The single malt that started it all". Today, the distillery is owned by the french alcoholic beverages company Pernod Ricard.

12. It is a distilled beverage made from Damson plums. It is frequently called plum brandy and is part of the category of drinks called rakia. Identify.

13. This company was established in 1843 and the same year, the founders got their royal warrant. This famous brand's name comes from Gaelic seamhas, meaning 'a narrow place in a river'. Identify.

14. A proprietary recipe is blended into the rum mixture at the final stages of production, making use of spices indigenous to the Caribbean Islands giving the brand its taste. It is named after the 17th-century Caribbean privateer from Wales. Identify the brand.

15. What is the term for a partially frozen, often fruity drink and usually a mixture of ingredients served over a mound of crushed ice? This term can now be found in items list of any coffee shop.

16. Which brand used the slogan "Born 1820 – Still going Strong!" in their commercials when James Stevenson joined the company as the managing director?

17. 'Whassup?' was a commercial campaign for which brand from 1999 to 2002? The commercial made 'Whassup' a part of American lingo.

?

18. This beer company was founded to cater to a market for less gassy lager. Its beer was first brewed in Bangalore in 1990 and imported to the UK, until in 1997; it commenced brewing under licence with Charles Wells in the UK. Which company?

> *In a testament to its long history and popularity, VB has acquired a number of nicknames, ranging from the abbreviated "Vic Bitter", polite "Very Best", "Vitamin B", "Veebs" and "Victory Beer".*

19. On 4 May 1951, Sir Hugh Beaver, then the MD of a brewery, went on a shooting party in North Slob, Ireland. He became involved in an argument over which was the fastest game bird in Europe. That evening at Castlebridge House, he realized that it was impossible to confirm the same from any reference book. This incident led to the development of what? The brewery's storehouse is Dublin's most popular tourist attraction.

20. Name the brand of vintage champagne that is named after a Benedictine monk who was an important quality pioneer for Champagne wine.

Answers

1. Whyte & Mackay
2. Brandy
3. Carlsberg
4. Black Label
5. Guinness
6. The Striding Man logo of Johnnie Walker
7. Amstel (Amsterdam gets its name from the Amstel river)
8. Vat 69
9. Bacardi
10. Mezcal
11. Glenlivet
12. Slivovitz
13. Chivas Regal
14. Captain Morgan
15. Frappé
16. Johnnie Walker
17. Budweiser beer
18. Cobra Beer
19. Guinness Book of Records
20. Dom Perignon

✠✠✠

Liquor and Liquer II

Questions

1. Which brand of blended Scotch whisky first produced by Matthew Gloag & Son Limited in 1897 and now produced by The Edrington Group is named after a group of birds from the order Galliformes?
2. The founders of which movement developed a program of spiritual and character development, the Twelve Steps?
3. What brand of vodka gained additional popularity as the brand endorsed by James Bond in the Bond movie 'Die Another Day'?

In 2009, the advertising agency Bartle Bogle Hegarty created a new short film, starring Robert Carlyle called The Man Who Walked Around the World, which outlined the history of the Johnnie Walker brand.

4. From which fruit is Grenadine, the popular syrup used as an ingredient in cocktails made?
5. Lynchburg is best known as the location of which whiskey's distillery, that is marketed world wide as the product of a city with only one traffic light?
6. A concoction of dry gin, dom benedictine, cointreau and cherry brandy, shaken up with lime and pineapple juices and a dash of angostura bitters and grenadines. Celebrated the world over, it was created in 1915 in a famous hotel. Which drink?
7. James Joyce suggested the following slogan for which brand "The free, the flow, the frothy freshner"?
8. It is a brand of fruit based uncarbonated soft drink produced by GlaxoSmithKline. The original and most common variety contains real blackcurrant juice. It was originally manufactured by the Timbuktu-based food and drink company HW Carter as a blackcurrant cordial. Which fruit based drink?
9. Which beer brand is known for its advertising campaign that was called the Stubby Symphony, where 100 members of the Melbourne

and Victorian orchestras play the theme from 'The Magnificent Seven' only using the brand's beer bottles?

10. In 2001, which company acquired the line of Seagram's mixers (ginger ale, tonic water, club soda and seltzer water) from Pernod Ricard and Diageo, as well as signing a long term agreement to use the Seagram's name from Pernod Ricard?

11. Alexander first introduced the iconic square bottle in 1870. The other identifying characteristic of the bottle is the label, which is applied at an angle of 24 degrees. Identify the brand whose bottle is being talked about.

Asia's first beer was 'Lion' launched by Kasauli Brewery established by Edward Dyer in 1885 under the name Dyer Breweries. It later merged with Meakin Breweries Limited to become Dyer Meakin Breweries Ltd. The company still exists today under the name Mohan Meakin Limited.

12. This brand of beer derives its name from a city in Southern Bohemia. It is one of the major breweries that emphasize humorous advertising campaigns such as the "Real Men of Genius" radio commercials. Which brand of beer?

13. Which South African brewing company is one of the world's largest Coca-Cola bottlers?

14. The Bronfman family is one of the most influential Jewish families in the world. It owes its initial fame to Samuel Bronfman, who made a fortune in the alcoholic distilled beverage business during the 20th century. The fortune was made through the means of a company. Identify the company.

15. Which company announced the acquisition of Sweden-based V&S Group including the Absolut Vodka in 2008?

16. Which was the favourite champagne of Sir Winston Churchill? After Churchill's death in 1965, they placed a black border around the labels of Brut NV shipped to the United Kingdom.

17. In the 2002 film 'Die Another Day', James Bond (played by Pierce Brosnan) is heard asking for a bottle of which champagne?

18. Which brand of Scotch whiskey owned by Berry Brothers & Rudd was named after a clipper ship built in 1869 in Scotland? The most popular member of the range is sold in a distinctive green bottle with a yellow label.

19. Which liquor is made from potatoes, literal meaning of which is 'little water'?

20. In 1886 Dr. H. Elion, a pupil of the French chemist Louis Pasteur, developed a yeast that is still used for this beer. Its main advertising slogan in the UK was "Refreshes the parts other beers cannot reach". Identify the beer brand.

Answers

1. The Famous Grouse
2. Alcoholics Anonymous
3. Findlandia
4. Pomegranate
5. Jack Daniel's
6. Singapore Sling
7. Guiness Beer
8. Ribena
9. Victoria Bitter
10. The Coca-Cola Company
11. Johnnie Walker
12. Budweiser beer; the city is Budweis.
13. SABMiller plc; the company was founded in South Africa in 1895 as South African Breweries.
14. Seagram
15. Pernod Ricard
16. Pol Roger
17. Bollinger
18. Cutty Sark
19. Vodka
20. Heineken

✠✠✠

Masthead

Questions

1. In 1928, which newspaper became the first newspaper distributed by airplane, flying copies to London from Paris in time for breakfast?
2. Name the British newspaper published on Sunday that started a campaign named 'Dignity at Home' to help elderly people.
3. Rudyard Kipling used to work as a correspondent for which newspaper?
4. This newspaper can be considered the French counterpart of the Wall Street Journal and Financial Times. The paper initially appeared under the auspices of textile traders Robert Schreiber and associate Albert Aronson and became a weekly in 1913. It is currently owned by London-based Pearson group who acquired it in 1989. Name this leading French newspaper.

Hickey's Bengal Gazette or the Calcutta General Advertiser was the first English language newspaper, and indeed the first printed newspaper, to be published in the Indian sub-continent.

5. What was started by PS Hariharan in 1961 and is characterised by its salmon-pink colour?
6. Which family is the former owner of Dow Jones & Company – publishers of the Wall Street Journal – which is now owned by Rupert Murdoch's News Corporation?
7. This term originally referred to the top of a tall vertical pole of a sailing ship which supports the sails. A brass plate would be affixed to the main mast of a commercial sailing vessel, which contained the name of the owners of the ship. Due to this reason, the term was borrowed in journalism to denote something that had a roughly similar purpose. What term?
8. What was founded in 1938 as a tutoring business for the New York State Regents Exam in the basement of the founder's Brooklyn home? In

1984, the founder sold the company to The Washington Post Company.

9. Which newspaper's reporters Bob Woodward and Carl Bernstein led the American media's investigation into what became known as the Watergate scandal?

10. 'A Life in Progress' is the autobiography of Canadian-born British historian and columnist who was for a time the third biggest newspaper magnate in the world and controlled Hollinger International, Inc. before investigation by regulators and investors. Identify the magnate.

11. A play by Pierre-Augustin Caron de Beaumarchais that was turned into a famous opera by Mozart contains a motto, "Sans la liberté de blâmer, il n'est point d'éloge flatteur" which translates as "Without the freedom to criticise, there is no true praise". This motto inspired the founding of which entity in 1826?

> *The term 'Gazette' gets its name from the name of a small copper coin in Venice. A monthly Government newspaper published in Venice in the mid-1500s was also known by the same name, because its price was one such copper coin.*

12. Every Thanksgiving the editorial page of this English-language international daily newspaper prints two famous articles that have appeared there since 1961. The first is titled "The Desolate Wilderness" and describes what the Pilgrims saw when they arrived at the Plymouth Colony. The second is titled "And the Fair Land" and describes in romantic terms the "bounty" of America. Which daily?

13. Which national American daily newspaper founded by Allen 'Al' Neuharth and published by the Gannett Company has received the derisive nickname 'McPaper'? The newspaper's motto, appearing on the top and bottom levels of the nameplate is 'The Nation's Newspaper - #1 in the USA'.

14. Which Indian daily was the first to own fleet of aircraft for distribution?

15. Which newspaper magnate's life inspired the Orson Welles film 'Citizen Kane'? He is known for originating yellow journalism along with Joseph Pulitzer.

16. Who is known to have purchased the New York World for $346,000 from Jay Gould in 1883?

17. Which newspaper was started in 1811 and directly descended from two newspapers – The Englishman and The Friend of India, both published from Kolkata?

18. Name the politician who was appointed executive editor of the Times of India in 1986 but was lured back to the Indian Express by Goenka in 1987.

19. Which daily was started by an Ayurvedic doctor and Congress Party member Varadarajulu Naidu in 1932 at Chennai but soon under financial difficulties was sold to S.Sadanand, founder of The Free Press Journal, then a national news agency?

20. What was founded by John Walter on 1 January 1785 as The Daily Universal Register, with Walter in the role of editor? It has gained the pompous/satirical nickname 'The Thunderer'.

Answers

1. The International Herald Tribune
2. Observer
3. The Pioneer
4. Les Echoes
5. The Economic Times
6. Bancroft family
7. Masthead
8. Kaplan Inc
9. The Washington Post
10. Conrad Black
11. Le Figaro, France's leading newspaper
12. The Wall Street Journal
13. USA Today; McPaper – A newspaper that is considered manu-factured and "for the masses" because of its simplistic prose style and flashy use of colours. Typically used in reference to USA Today.
14. The Hindu
15. William Randolph Hearst
16. Joseph Pulitzer
17. The Statesman
18. Arun Shourie
19. The Indian Express
20. The Times

✠✠✠

Quality Control

Questions

1. Which technique was first used by the Ford Motor Company as described explicitly by Henry Ford's My Life and Work (1923): "We have found in buying materials that it is not worthwhile to buy for other than immediate needs. We buy only enough to fit into the plan of production, taking into consideration the state of transportation at the time."

2. Recognising that the U.S. productivity was declining, President Reagan signed a legislation mandating a national conference on productivity in October 1982. The American Productivity and Quality Centre sponsored seven computer networking conferences in 1983 to prepare for an upcoming White House Conference on Productivity. This event led to the institution of what?

The particulars of six sigma methodology were first formulated by Bill Smith at Motorola in 1986.

3. According to Taiichi Ohno, the man credited with developing JIT, what is the means through which JIT is achieved?

4. Who once said: "There are 3 religions in Japan – Buddhism, Shintoism and Kaizen"?

5. Whom did Peter Drucker describe as: "He was the first man in recorded history who deemed work deserving of systematic observation and study. On his 'scientific management' rests, above all, the tremendous surge of affluence in the last seventy-five years which has lifted the working masses in the developed countries well above any level recorded before, even for the well-to-do."

6. What was instituted by the Bureau of Indian Standards in 1991, with a view to encourage Indian manufacturing and service organizations to strive for excellence and giving special recognition to those who are considered to be the leaders of quality movement in India? Shilpa Shetty was the recipient of this in the year 2007.

7. It is a theory of management that analyses and synthesises workflow processes, improving labour productivity. The core ideas of the theory were developed by Frederick Winslow Taylor in the 1880s and 1890s, and were first published in his monographs and Shop Management (1905). Which theory of management?

8. "As a statistician, he was, like so many of the rest of us, self-taught, on a good background of physics and mathematics." About whom did Deming say this?

9. Who was featured prominently in an NBC documentary titled 'If Japan can... Why can't we?' about the increasing industrial competition the United States was facing from Japan in 1980?

10. What name has GE given to the senior managers who actually define the projects under Six Sigma?

> *The term kanban describes an embellished wooden or metal sign often representing a trademark or seal.*

11. Business management thinker Joseph M. Juran suggested this principle and named it after an Italian economist. Identify the principle.

12. What according to Deming is 'predictable degree of uniformity and dependability, at low cost and suited to the market'?

13. It is known as a fishbone diagram because of its shape, being similar to the side view of a fish skeleton. Mazda Motors famously used this in the development of the Miata sports car, where the required result was "Jinba Ittai" or "Horse and Rider as One". Name the quality guru behind this diagram.

14. It is a Japanese term that means "fail-safing", "foolproof" or "mistake-proofing" – a method of preventing errors by putting limits on how an operation can be performed in order to force the correct completion of the operation. The concept was formalised, and the term adopted by Shigeo Shingo as part of the Toyota Production System. Which term?

IDENTIFY THE QUALITY GURUS IN QUESTION 15-20.

15. He worked at Western Electric from 1924 to 1941. He travelled to Japan in 1954 to teach quality management. His trilogy for managing quality is carried out by the three interrelated processes of planning, control and improvement. He is known for his 'Quality Control Handbook'.

16. He developed his loss function concept that combines cost, target and variation into one metric.

17. In 1952, he authored 'Total Quality Control'. He argues that total quality control is necessary to achieve productivity, market penetration and competitive advantage.

18. He spent his professional career at Western Electric and Bell Telephone Laboratories, both divisions of AT&T. He developed the control chart theory. In 1931, he authored 'Economic Control of Manufactured Product'. He hase also developed the PDSA cycle for learning and improvement.

19. His first book 'Quality is Free' sold 1.5 million copies and changed the way management looked at quality. He argued that 'doing it right the first time' is less expensive than the costs of detecting and correcting non-conformities. He hase also the author of the book 'Quality Without Tears'.

20. He was a protégé of Shewart. He taught statistical process control and the importance of quality to the leading CEOs of Japanese industry. His 14 point provides a theory for management to improve quality and productivity.

Answers

1. Just-in-time (JIT)
2. Malcolm Baldrige National Quality Award
3. Kanban
4. Masaaki Imai
5. Frederick W. Taylor
6. Rajiv Gandhi National Quality Award
7. Scientific management
8. Walter Andrew Shewart
9. W. Edwards Deming
10. Champions
11. Pareto Principle
12. Quality
13. Kaoru Ishikawa
14. Poka-yoke
15. Joseph M. Juran
16. Genichi Taguchi
17. Armand V. Fiegenbaum
18. Walter A. Shewart
19. Phillip B. Crosby
20. W. Edwards Deming

✠ ✠ ✠

Quench Your Thirst: The World of Beverages

Questions

1. Name the company founded by Johann Jacob which made heavy use of onomatopoeia in their commercials after the sound of the gas escaping as one opens the bottle.

2. Ray Graves, coach of a football team, was frustrated with the performance of his players during the hot summer football practices, and asked the team doctor for his insight. This incident led to the development of which sports drink?

3. Fresh-Up Freddie was the rooster mascot for which brand in 1950s? He gave viewers lessons about how to plan successful parties and picnics.

4. Name the Pepsi brand that was originally marketed as "zero proof moonshine" and had pictures of hillbillies on the bottle until 1973.

5. Which company promised every man in uniform its product for 5 cents, wherever he was during the World War II?

Campa Cola was a drink created by the Pure Drinks Group in the 1970s that was the market leader in most regions of India for a period spanning several years until the advent of the foreign players Pepsi and Coca-Cola after the liberalisation policy of the P. V. Narasimha Rao Government in 1991.

6. Which brand name of tea has its origin in a legend when a Buddhist monk visited the tea gardens and exclaimed that the brand name meant `thus far and no further'?

7. Under Robert Woodruff, Coke changed its formula so that the glycerine used in the syrup came not from hog fat but from vegetable sources. For what specific reason was this done?

8. A popular beverage gets its name from a Greek Athlete who was reputed to have phenomenal strength. He was said to have supported

the roof of a collapsing building in which the mathematician, Pythagoras, was teaching, thus saving his life. Name the beverage.

9. Following the 2002 boycott of Coca-Cola by Saudi Arabia, it was unofficially dubbed the soft drink of the Hajj. The product's name is a reference to a well in Mecca, that is one of the stops on the Islamic pilgrimage of the Hajj. However, it is not made with water from the well. Which soft drink?

10. This man was a surgeon during the American Civil War, and later settled down in Rural Retreat, Virginia. One of his employees, Wade Morrison, went on to found a beverage brand and named it after him. Which brand?

The Los Angeles based band Goldspot is named after a fizzy drink of the same name.

11. Which drink owes its origin to a major breakthrough in 1954, when Anthony T. Rossi invented and patented a pasteurization process to aseptically pack pure chilled juice in glass bottles, allowing it to be shipped and stored without refrigeration? "Juice Train" is one of the innovations of this brand for distribution. Seagram's owned this drink from 1986 to 1998.

12. When the post-emergency Indian government banned Coca-Cola, what alternative drink was introduced and named after its year of introduction? George Fernandes was responsible for banning the American soft drink giant along with IBM from India.

13. Which fruit-based drink was formulated by the German Coca-Cola bottling company due to shipping restrictions between the US and Germany during World War II when the German plant could not get Coca-Cola syrup?

14. When this brand's founder had visited Bangkok in 1982 on a business trip, he found that a local brand Krating Daeng helped cure his jet lag. The founder adapted this drink for the European market and launched it as a new brand. Which brand resulted?

15. Which eponymous brand of tea was founded in the early 17th century after the founder bought Tom's Coffee house in London and set up operations?

16. Which drink was first sold at Jacobs' Pharmacy for five cents a glass?

17. The Coca-Cola Company have stated that 'X' is the main competitor to Coca-Cola rather than the Pepsi. Identify X.

18. Known for his catchphrase "Oh yeah!", he is a gigantic anthropomorphic pitcher, filled with a popular drink and marked with a finger painted smiley face. Who is he?

19. According to Professor Donald Sadoway (MIT), the name of this beverage is derived from the atomic mass of Lithium which was originally one of the key ingredients of the drink (as lithium citrate). Which beverage?

20. Which drink was appointed to the Royal Household of the Governor General of Canada, seeing the change in the label from a beaver atop a map to the present Crown and shield in 1907? Canadian pharmacist John J. McLaughlin is the formulator of this drink.

Answers

1. Schweppes; the sound was "Schhhhh.... Schweppes"
2. Gatorade; the Florida Gators was the football team
3. 7Up
4. Mountain Dew
5. The Coca-Cola Company
6. Runglee Rungliot
7. To ensure it could be certified as kosher
8. Milo
9. Zam Zam Cola
10. Dr Pepper
11. Tropicana
12. 77 cola
13. Fanta
14. Red Bull
15. Twinings
16. Coca-Cola
17. Robinson Barley
18. Kool-Aid Man
19. 7Up
20. Canada Dry

✠ ✠ ✠

Quote Unquote

Questions

1. Who famously told the following lines to his sales people "The trouble with every one of us is that we don't think enough. We don't get paid for working with our feet – we get paid for working with our heads. Any man on the selling force could make two dollars where he now makes one if he would think along the right lines. "I don't think" has cost the world millions of dollars."

2. "I would have been fired a hundred times at a company run by MBAs. But I never went into business to make money. I went into business so that I could do interesting things that hadn't been done before." Whose words?

3. The founder of which brand once said, "I have done more than anyone else to change the face of mankind"?

4. Which Indian fashion designers said, 'We don't make garments, we make heirlooms'?

5. Change management is huge concept globally these days and in 2007, the most quoted quote about change management was, "Be the change you want to see in the world." Who said this quote about change management?

6. Who said the following about gold in 1998 at Harvard? "It gets dug out of the ground in Africa, or someplace. Then we melt it down, dig another hole, bury it again and pay people to stand around guarding it. It has no utility. Anyone watching from Mars would be scratching their head."

7. Which eccentric hotel owner said, "We don't pay taxes only the little people pay taxes"?

8. Who said - "Most everything I have done I've copied from someone else"?

9. "The success of any advertisement whether of a business or political nature depends on the consistency and perseverance with which it is employed," is a famous statement of which personality?

10. "If you are not the number one in the world, you cannot be number one in Japan" is whose favourite saying?

11. "So we went to Atari and said, 'Hey, we've got this amazing thing, even built with some of your parts, and what do you think about funding us? Or we'll give it to you. We just want to do it. Pay our salary; we'll come work for you.' And they said, 'No.' So then we went to Hewlett – Packard and they said, 'Hey, we don't need you. You haven't got through college yet." Whose words were these and what amazing thing was he talking about?

12. Whose words: "What can I say? I hired the wrong guy. He destroyed everything I spent 10 years working for; starting with me, but that wasn't the saddest part. I would have gladly left Apple if Apple would have turned out like I wanted it to"?

13. In an interview for 'Harper's Bazaar' in 1923, who said, 'I gave women a sense of freedom; I gave them back their bodies: bodies that were drenched in sweat, due to fashion's finery, lace, corsets, underclothes, padding'?

14. "A Coke is a Coke, and no amount of money can get you a better Coke than the one, the bum on the corner is drinking. All the Cokes are the same and all the Cokes are good. Liz Taylor knows it, the President knows it, the bum knows it, and you know it." To which artist is this quote attributed?

15. Which famous economist said "There is no art which one government learns from another faster than that of draining money from the pockets of the people"?

16. Which famous retailer said, "There is only one boss, the customer, and he can fire everybody in the company, from the chairman or down, simply by spending his money somewhere else"?

17. "The best thing that happened to me was joining Intel and the best thing that happened to me was leaving Intel." Which Indian Silicon Valley legend said this on leaving Intel?

18. Whose quote about the cigarette business: "I'll tell you why I like the cigarette business. It costs a penny to make. Sell it for a dollar. It's addictive. And there's fantastic brand loyalty"?

19. "I don't think I printed two issues and they weren't much. However, this experience did impress me with the difficulty of getting words into hard copy, and this, in turn, started me thinking about duplicating processes. I started a little inventor's notebook, and I would jot down ideas from time to time." Identify the inventor.

20. "A fellow kept hanging around my hotel waving $300 at me and saying that he wanted to put the mouse on paper tablets for school children. As usual, Roy and I needed money, so I took the $300." Whose words?

Answers

1. Thomas John Watson, Sr
2. Amar Bose
3. Gillette
4. Abu Jani and Sandeep Khosla
5. Mahatma Gandhi
6. Warren Buffet
7. Leona Helmsey
8. Sam Walton
9. Adolf Hitler
10. Honda
11. Steve Jobs about the personal computer he made along with Steve Woznaik.
12. Steve Jobs about John Sculley
13. Coco Chanel
14. Andy Warhol
15. Adam Smith
16. Sam Walton
17. Vinod Dham
18. Warren Buffett
19. Chester Carlson
20. Walt Disney

✠✠✠

The Fast Movers: FMCG

Questions

1. The first known reference to this name was by the inventor Robert Chesebrough in his U.S. patent. He coined this name because he used his wife's flower vases to store the product. Which name?

2. What was designed and patented by Dr. Robert Hutson, a California periodontist in 1950?

3. The company's mission to provide "Better Products, Better Value, Better Living". In November, 2007, the company purchased the American raw materials company Searles Valley Minerals Inc. Identify the company.

4. What was created by an English bakery Peek Freans in London in 1874 to commemorate the marriage of the Grand Duchess Maria Alexandrovna of Russia to the Duke of Edinburgh? It became popular throughout Europe, particularly in Spain where, following the Spanish Civil War, it became a symbol of Spain's economic recovery after bakers produced mass quantities to consume a surplus of wheat.

An Oral-B toothbrush is the first to go to the moon. It rode on the Apollo 11 mission.

5. Which world-famous candy bar, more than 70 years old, was named after a horse owned by the company's founding family?

6. Which soap brand derives its name from the chemical Synthetic Phenol? The name of the company that owns the brand derives its name from an important tribe in Iran.

7. It exits the iconic glass bottle at .028 miles per hour. If its viscosity is greater than this speed, it is rejected for sale. Quality standards for which product has been described above?

8. The original name of this product was "LR Croup and Pneumonia Salve". Its founder's son thought that the name was too cumbersome

and renamed it after his brother-in-law, who was a doctor. Identify the brand.

9. Which popular skin care brand owned by Reckitt Benckiser was invented by Ivan Combe in 1950?

10. The herbalist, Aw Chu Kin, told his sons to develop this product in his deathbed in the 1870s in Rangoon. Interestingly, the producers of this item also started three of the first few theme parks in Asia – Hong Kong, Singapore and Fujian. Identify this product, which comes in 2 colours – red and white.

11. Which company received its Royal Warrant in 1854 as "manufacturers of cocoa and chocolate to Queen Victoria"?

12. This company's list of well-known clientele for its oleochemicals business include Clariant, BASF and Huntsman. It also manufactures personal care products on contract basis for leading national and multinational brands such as Dabur (Vatika), Henkel (Fa), Reckitt Benckiser (Dettol), Beirsdorf (Nivea). It also has its own soap brands with the name Doy. Identify the company.

Wrigley's Juicy Fruit gum was the first product to be scanned using a UPC bar code.

13. In 1869, Henry and Clarence launched this company, whose first product was "Henry's mother's pure and superior grated horseradish, bottled in clear glass to show its purity." Which company was started by the duo?

14. Name the famous brand of tissue, now owned by P&G, which was first created in 1928 by the Hoberg Paper Company. This brand is famous for its advertising icon Mr Whipple, once polled as the third 'most recognised man' in the US in the 1970s.

15. This brand of common salt used the slogan, 'When it pours, it rains'. The "Umbrella Girl" associated with this brand has gone through six different iterations within advertising campaigns. Name the brand.

16. Which brand's name figures in the title of the biography of William Lever authored by Adam Macqueen?

17. While working as a traveling salesman for the Crown Cork and Seal Company to support his family, he saw bottle caps, with the cork seal he sold, thrown away after opening the 'bottle. This made him realise the value in basing a business on a disposable product. He is known for a unique business model that later became known as freebie marketing. Who has been described?

18. Which company was the original producer of Old Spice that was founded in 1934 by William Lightfoot Schultz?

19. Ronald Reagan was a spokesman for which beverage owned by Campbell Soup Company when it was first introduced?

20. Its name is believed to have come from an early 18th Century English club in London with strong political and literary associations. It was developed after a worker at the company's factory in York put a suggestion in the suggestion box for a snack that a 'man could have in his lunch box for work'. Name the brand and the company.

Answers

1. Vaseline
2. Oral-B toothbrush
3. Nirma
4. Marie Biscuits
5. Snickers
6. Cinthol; the name Godrej is derived from Guderz – an important tribe in Iran.
7. Heinz
8. Vicks Vaporub
9. Clearsil
10. Tiger Balm
11. Cadbury
12. VVF Limited
13. Heinz Ketchup
14. Charmin
15. Morton Salt
16. Sunlight
17. King Camp Gillette
18. Shulton Company
19. V8 vegetable soup
20. Kit Kat and Rowntree

✠✠✠

The Glossy World

Questions

1. What was created in 1923 by Briton Hadden and Henry Luce, featuring Joseph G. Cannon, the retired Speaker of the US House of Representatives on its cover? Arvind Adiga worked as a correspondent for 3 years for this news magazine.

2. Name the magazine that was launched in 1931 in the United States as Apparel Arts and is closely associated with metrosexuality.

3. Which British magazine was founded on 17 July 1841 by Henry Mayhew and Ebenezer Landells and was initially sub titled "The London Charivari"?

4. Which publication was founded by James Wilson, a hat maker from the small Scottish town of Hawick, who believed in free trade, internationalism and minimum interference by government, especially in the affairs of the market?

5. The 'September Issue' is a documentary film about the behind-the-scenes drama that follows editor-in-chief of this magazine and her staff during the production of the 'September 2007' issue. Due to the popularity of the film, the issue that was documented in the film has peaked to prices between $80 and $115 on eBay, making it one of the most sought after issues of the magazine. Identify the magazine.

At the first MAD art auction, long-time MAD fans Steven Spielberg and George Lucas purchased the original art for 11 covers of Mad featuring spoofs of their movies. Spielberg also bought the cover of MAD #1.

6. Name the publishing company that owns the content aggregation site – reddit.

7. Name the men's magazine that published "For Rupert – with no promises" as an unsigned work of fiction in 1977; this was the first time it had published a work without identifying the author.

8. The first issue of this magazine published in the US in 1894 had

the declaration on its ornate opening page that it was "devoted to the interests of advertisers, poster printers, bill posters, advertising agents and secretaries of fairs." Name it.

9. Which automobile magazine published by BBC Worldwide is named after BBC's television show?

10. Which magazine's mascot, Alfred E. Neuman, is typically the focal point of the magazine's cover, with his face often replacing a celebrity or character that is lampooned within the issue?

11. Which publication was founded by Time co-founder Henry Luce in February 1930, four months after the Wall Street Crash of 1929 that marked the onset of the Great Depression?

12. Which magazine, first published in August 1954 by Henry Luce of Time, aspired to be "not a sports magazine, but the sports magazine."?

The first "Word Power" was published in the January 1945 edition of Reader's Digest. The author's name, Wilfred Funk, was disclosed in the February 1945 issue.

13. This magazine, which calls itself a newspaper, was first published in 1843 to "take part in a severe contest between intelligence, which presses forward, and an unworthy, timid ignorance obstructing our progress." Which magazine?

14. He is the only U.S. President since Herbert Hoover to not be named Time Magazine's Person of the Year during his term and was once a cover model for Cosmopolitan Magazine. Who is he?

15. It was first published in 11 January 1902 by H. H. Windsor, and has been owned since 1958 by the Hearst Corporation. A recurring column in this magazine is "Jay Leno's Garage" featuring observations by the famed late-night talk show host and vehicle enthusiast. Identify the American magazine.

16. Which magazine was started by a Scottish immigrant Bertie Charles who came to New York in 1904 and got his first job by offering to work for nothing as a reporter for The Journal of Commerce?

17. 2005: America in your pocket
2008: Life well shared
Identify the publication.

18. Launched by Hathway Investments Private Limited, this weekly newsmagazine is currently owned by the Rajan Raheja Group. Tarun Tejpal is a past editor of the magazine. Identify.

19. Which monthly general-interest family magazine was co-founded in 1922 by Lila Bell Wallace and DeWitt Wallace?

20. Name the magazine that was founded by Bob Guccione in the 1990s. It is owned by FriendFinder Network, formerly known as General Media Inc.

Answers

1. Time Magazine
2. GQ
3. Punch
4. The Economist
5. Vogue
6. Condé Nast
7. Esquire
8. Billboard
9. Top Gear
10. Mad magazine
11. Fortune
12. Sports Illustrated
13. The Economist
14. Gerald Ford
15. Popular Mechanics
16. Forbes
17. Reader's Digest
18. Outlook
19. Reader's Digest
20. Penthouse

✠✠✠

You Deserve a Break Today

Questions

1. Name the UK-based chain of hamburger restaurants that gets its name from the Popeye cartoons created by Elzie Crisler Segar.

2. This university is on an 80 acre campus. 19 full-time international resident instructors teach students from more than 119 countries. The state-of-the-art facility includes 13 teaching rooms, a 300 seat auditorium, 12 interactive education team rooms, and 3 kitchen labs. Identify the university.

3. In 1972, they started the tradition of celebrating every Thursday night like a New Year's Eve party, with champagne, confetti and noisemakers. Identify.

4. On 1 April 1996, which restaurant chain took out a fullpage advertisement in The New York Times announcing that they had purchased the Liberty Bell to "reduce the country's debt" and renamed it? Thousands of people who did not immediately understand the press release as an April Fool's Day hoax protested.

5. What was founded in 1937 by Shivkisan Agrawal, as retail sweets and namkeens shop in Bikaner, Rajastan?

6. It shares its name with a song recorded by The Rolling Stones in 1966. In April 1982, it became part of the Specialty Restaurant Division of Morrison Inc. Name this American casual dining restaurant chain that began re-branding itself, moving out of the "bar-and-grill" segment of the industry in 2007.

7. Name the chain of fast-food restaurants founded by partners Roy Allen and Frank Wright, currently owned by Yum! Brands, that is distinguished by its draft root beer and root beer floats.

☀ *Hard Rock Café has been owned by the Seminole Tribe of Florida since 2006.*

8. Founded in 1971 by Isaac Tigrett and Peter Morton, this café was reportedly named after an album of 'The Doors'. Their motto 'Love All, Serve All' was adopted from Tigrett's guru Sathya Sai Baba. Which café?

9. It was a brainchild of Robert Earl, former president of Hard Rock Cafe and was launched in New York in 1991, with the backing of Hollywood stars Sylvester Stallone, Bruce Willis, Demi Moore, and Arnold Schwarzenegger. Identify the theme restaurant chain.

10. Italian brothers Sergio and Bruno set up their coffee roastery in London in 1971 giving rise to a coffee house company where the employees will tell you that "Making coffee is an art". Identify the company.

11. Their first restaurant featured a red-and-white striped awning, and blue paint, and the interior included wooden floors, bentwood chairs, and striped tablecloth. The company licenses its name to Heinz for snack items and frozen foods sold in grocery stores. Identify the company.

12. If you were using a Lazy Suzy or a lazy Susan, what would you be doing?

13. Who waged war on its competitors claiming that taste tests showed its Whopper to be the choice of American consumers in 1982?

In 1997, former Soviet Union Premier Mikhail Gorbachev starred in a Pizza Hut commercial to raise money for the Perestroyka Archives.

14. Which brand uses the term the third place in its marketing because it vies to be the "extra place" people frequent after home and work?

15. Dave Thomas stressed that each of Wendy's employees should have an "MBA". What is an MBA?

16. Anderson is credited with invention of "the kitchen as assembly line, and the cook as infinitely replaceable technician", hence giving rise to the modern fast food phenomenon. He had developed an efficient method for cooking hamburgers, using freshly ground beef and fresh onions. Which chain did Anderson start ?

17. Which company was created in 1997, as Tricon Global Restaurants Inc. as a result of a spin-off from PepsiCo?

18. Name the brainchild unit of RK Group, which resumed 35 years ago, started their career from railway catering business.

19. Which fast-food restaurant chain's name and concept was inspired by Robert Louis Stevenson's book Treasure Island?

20. Which Italy-based, multinational catering and retail company is the world's largest in the travel dining sector and derives over 90% of the its business from outlets in airport terminals and motorway service areas?

Answers

1. Wimpy
2. Hamburger University
3. T.G.I. Friday's
4. Taco Bell
5. Haldiram
6. Ruby Tuesday
7. A&W Restaurants Inc.
8. Hard Rock Cafe
9. Planet Hollywood
10. Costa Coffee
11. T.G.I. Friday's
12. Eating at a Chinese restaurant – a Lazy Suzy is the revolving table-top.
13. Burger King
14. Starbucks
15. A mop bucket attitude, that stressed cleanliness and customer services.
16. White Castle
17. YUM! Brands
18. Comesum Food Plaza
19. Long John Silver's
20. Autogrill

✠ ✠ ✠

Section II
Questions

Potpourri I

Questions

1. The idea for what is believed to be conceived by E. M. Stuart who proposed it as a means to "maintain the glory of a community whose name means glamour and excitement in the four corners of the world"?

2. When asked what she wore in bed, who is said to have replied thus: "Two drops of Chanel No. 5"?

3. Which company traces its history back to 1860, with the publication by Henry Varnum Poor of History of Railroads and Canals in the United States? It is a division of The McGraw-Hill Companies that publishes financial research and analysis on stocks and bonds.

4. Who reconstructed version of Edison's invention factory in Dearborn, Michigan, to celebrate Light's Golden Jubilee?

5. Which company was established as Takachiho Seisakusho on 12 October 1919? The current name of the company is named after the home of the 12 supreme gods and goddesses in Greek mythology.

The patent for the famous mold used for making Toblerone chocolates was given by Albert Einstein.

6. Who was the director of the Lehar Pepsi launch advertisement featuring Remo Fernandes and Juhi Chawla?

7. Which is the first hotel in the world to be registered by the UNFCCC for carbon emission reductions?

8. What was the name of the first practical car radio developed by Bill Lear and Elmer Wavering in the 1920s?

9. Which company's origins are in the 1940 Honolulu based company called Standard Games?

10. Which company owes its origin to the founder's aunt who asked him about a book for crossword puzzles that she could gift to a friend?

11. Who is best known for the Easter eggs made using precious metals and gemstones rather than mundane materials?

12. The idea for which brand name struck to its founder by observing chickens in his yard and demonstrated the way his arch supports worked by keeping a chicken foot on his office desk?

13. Who founded the Pittsburgh-based Duquesne Amusement & Supply Company to distribute films in 1904?

14. What was founded in London on 11 March 1744 when Samuel Baker presided over the disposal of "several hundred scarce and valuable" books from the library of a certain Rt. Hon. Sir John Stanley?

> *The original product of Nintendo when it was established was Hanafuda, Japanese playing cards.*

15. Which stock exchange, set up in 1602 by 'Verenigde Oostindische Compagnie,' is considered the oldest in the world?

16. Often called a "YouTube for documents," it was originally inspired when Trip Adler was at Harvard and had a conversation with his father, John R. Adler about the difficulties of publishing academic papers. Identify.

17. President Theodore Roosevelt referred to him as a "superb portrait of the common man". He inspired a Broadway musical Helen of Troy in 1923. Who is he?

18. What is the name of the front company for MI6 agents in James Bond movies?

19. The logo for the brand prominently features a Basset Hound whose real name is Jason. Identify the brand.

20. The name of which American media conglomerate founded in 1972 by Lowry Mays and Red McCombs comes from AM broadcasting, referring to a channel (frequency) on which only one station transmits in U.S. and Canadian broadcasting history?

Answers

1. Hollywood Walk of Fame
2. Marlyn Monroe
3. Standard & Poor's
4. Henry Ford
5. Olympus
6. Vidhu Vinod Chopra
7. ITC Sonar, Kolkata
8. Motorola
9. SEGA
10. Simon & Schuster
11. Peter Carl Fabergé
12. New Balance Shoes
13. Warner Brothers
14. Sotheby's
15. Amsterdam Stock Exchange
16. Scribd
17. The Arrow Collar Man
18. Universal Exports
19. Hush Puppies
20. Clear Channel Communications

✠✠✠

Potpourri II

Questions

1. Name the world's costliest coffee priced at $130 a pound. It is in the droppings of a type of marsupial that eats only the very best coffee beans. Plantation workers track them and scoop their precious poop.

2. Which road in New York, named after the fourth president of the US, is associated with the American advertising industry?

3. Scientist Samuel Ruben and a manufacturer of tungsten filament wire named Philip Rogers Mallory were the people behind which famous brand?

4. Who once said that he has made more money from his grilling machine contracts than he made during his entire boxing career, and has suggested that he's better known for the grill than he is for his boxing?

5. What appeared for the first time in the newspaper 'Belle life in London' in 1835?

6. Which portal was created in 1999 by the merger of TMB and Online Career Center (OCC)?

7. This company's core business was the manufacturing of headphones. If the headphones came through quality tests, the company would give the headphones a blue dot. The quality symbol became a trademark and the trademark became the company's name in 1938. Name the company.

> When the first Indian explorers reached Antarctica in 1987, they raised the Indian flag on a pedestal built with a special cement developed by ACC that could set under extreme sub-zero conditions.

8. Which famous surname literally means 'iron smith' in Italian?

9. Who made the first cover design of Jawaharlal Nehru's "The Discovery of India"?

10. It is characterized by green flashing reversed Roman and Japanese katakana characters and Arabic numerals, as well as pictorial symbols, such as a bull's head falling in a black screen while changing and fading. The effect resembles that of the older green screen displays, since the letters leave a fluorescent trace on the screen. Identify.

11. About which movie did Val Kilmer remark "It was a one-dimensional cartoon which sold a lot of Ray Bans?"

12. The concept of what originates with the Statute of Anne (1710) in Britain? It was created as an act "for the encouragement of learning".

13. Name the detergent brand which got its name from its ingredients: Sodium Perborate and Silicate.

14. How do we better know 'The Shwayder Trunk Manufacturing Company'?

15. It is a popular comic strip created by Murat Bernard "Chic" Young and syndicated by King Features Syndicate. Chic Young drew the comic strip until his death in 1973, when the control of the strip passed to his son Dean Young. Name the comic strip.

16. Who started his career as an engineer with the Edison Illuminating Company in 1891?

17. I founded a human space flight startup company called Blue Origin in 2004. Artificial Artificial Intelligence (AAI) is a term coined by me. Who am I?

18. Name the organisation that was founded in May 1993 through the initiative of Peter Eigena and publishes an annual Corruption Perceptions Index, a comparative listing of corruption worldwide.

19. Danjaq LLC is the holding company responsible for the copyright and trademarks to the characters, elements, and other material related to which fictional character?

20. What was founded when a Swiss businessman Henry Dunant witnessed the Battle of Solferino and was shocked by the terrible aftermath of the battle?

Answers

1. Kopi Luwak
2. Madison Avenue
3. Duracell
4. George Edward Foreman
5. The first chess column
6. Monster.com
7. Blaukpunkt
8. Ferrari
9. Satyajit Ray
10. Matrix Code
11. Top Gun
12. Copyright
13. Persil
14. Samsonite
15. Blondie
16. Henry Ford
17. Jeff Bezoz
18. Transparency International
19. James Bond
20. Red Cross

✠✠✠

Potpourri III

Questions

1. Which term was coined by the US soldiers after World War II, presumably because they had trouble pronouncing its original name 'Offiziersmesser'?

2. Originally it was knows as Mohammedan Anglo-Oriental College, founded by a Muslim social reformer Sir Syed Ahmed Khan. Identify.

3. Which company was established in April 1946 by an engineer specializing in fabrication technology? The first major product of the company was the yubiwa pipe, a finger ring that would hold a cigarette.

4. What was founded in 1966 in New York City by A.C. Bhaktivedanta Swami Prabhupada?

5. Otis Elevator entered Indian markets through a joint venture with which Indian company in 1953?

6. My catalogue, known as the "Blue Book", was published in 1845. It is still being published today. Who am I?

7. What was described by Steve Jobs as the conceptual forerunner of the World Wide Web, stating that it was "sort of like Google in paperback form, 35 years before Google came along"?

Daily Planet is a licensed brothel in Melbourne, Australia. It entered the news in 2003 when it became one of the first brothels listed on a stock exchange.

8. Who gained recognition for his design after he was contracted to provide clothing styles for the movie The Great Gatsby?

9. Who began his service as a consultant to Transcontinental Air Transport and Pan American Airways in 1928?

10. Whirlpool forayed into the Indian markets under a joint venture with which Indian group?

11. Which great writer and poet introduced and promoted the sport of Judo in India?

12. Gautam Hari Singhania, Chairman & Managing Director of Raymond group, was instrumental in the successful launch of which brand in 1991 in India?

13. Which watch brand timed the solo flight made by Charles Lindbergh from New York to Paris in 1927?

14. Which toy brand did the US Postal Service choose to use on its commemorative stamp celebrating the 100th anniversary of the naming of the teddy bear in 2002?

15. It was a newspaper column that began running in the New York Globe in 1918. It originally documented sporting feats, and was called 'Champs and Chumps', before its present name was adopted. It was later adapted to radio, television and book formats. What is being referred to?

The album 'Beyond Time' by Jagjit Singh is the first digitally recorded album of India. It was recorded in the studio 'Western outdoor' by sound recordists duo Daman Sood and Avinash Oak.

16. Which company has a 'Simplicity Advisory Board' that brings together five experts from the worlds of healthcare, lifestyle and technology?

17. Paws Inc. was founded in 1981 by Jim Davis for the licensing of which comic strip?

18. Which firm founded in 1976 by people who had previously worked together at Bear Stearns, was responsible for the 1988 leveraged buyout of RJR Nabisco?

19. Canada-based Harlequin Enterprises, owned by the Torstar Corporation, has set up a subsidiary in India to print and distribute which well-known fiction brand?

20. What system was introduced by Indian post on 15 August 1972 that considerably speeded up and eased delivery?

Answers

1. Swiss Army knife
2. Aligarh Muslim University
3. Casio
4. International Society for Krishna Consciousness (ISKCON).
5. Mahindra & Mahindra
6. Tiffany & Co
7. Whole Earth Catalog
8. Ralph Lauren
9. Charles Lindbergh
10. TVS
11. Rabindranath Tagore
12. Kamasutra Condoms
13. Longines
14. Gund Bear
15. Ripley's Believe It or Not
16. Philips
17. Garfield
18. KKR
19. Mills & Boon
20. Postal Code

✠✠✠

Potpourri IV

Questions

1. Which company derives its name from the German word for 'air' and a powerful medieval trading group?
2. What was started on 15 April 1999 by Brad Fitzpatrick as a way of keeping his high school friends updated on his activities?
3. A film by Alexis Spraic titled 'Shadow Billionaire' documents the legal hoopla that took place after the death of one of the founders of which company?
4. Author of the novel 'The House of Blue Mangoes', became one of the founding members of Penguin in India. Who is he?
5. Which company can trace its beginning to the creation in May 1912 of the Famous Players Film Company?
6. Under the slogan "direct from the tea gardens to the tea pot", this Scottish entrepreneurial businessman wanted to make tea a popular and approachable drink for everyone – with a high quality but reasonably priced product. He was knighted by Queen Victoria who gave him the title of 'Sir' in 1898. Identify this Scottish entrepreneur.

Claiborne is best known for founding Liz Claiborne Inc. which in 1986 became the first company founded by a woman to make to the Fortune 500.

7. Who produces the 'Gold Bunny', a hollow milk chocolate rabbit in a variety of sizes available every Easter?
8. Founded by Margaretha and Wolfgang Ley in 1978 in Munich, the company was bought over by Megha Mittal, in November 2009. Identify.
9. Which company released a pair of goggles called the O-Frame in 1980?
10. In the early 1950s, Brooklyn-born toy inventor George Lerner came up with the idea of inserting small, pronged body and face parts into

fruits and vegetables to create a "funny face man." Which American toy got created as a result of this idea?

11. The company was founded in 1945 by Fritz and seven fellow engineers of the University of Hannover in a laboratory called Laboratorium Wennebostel named after the village of Wennebostel, where it had been moved due to the war. Its first product was a voltmeter. It began building microphones in 1946. The company has partnered with the Bollywood music director trio Shankar-Ehsaan-Loy to promote their brand. Which company?

Oakley was started by James Jannard in 1975 in his garage with an initial investment of $300 and was named after Jannard's dog, an English Setter.

12. Great Ormond Street Hospital for Sick Children holds the copyright for which fictional 'little boy'?

13. Which company traces its origin to the time when its founder Nathan Swartz bought part of the Abington Shoe Company and became sole owner of the company?

14. Which musical became the longest running Broadway musical, with 7,486 performances, overtaking Cats on 9 January 2006?

15. With which international appliance brand would you associate the line, "Our repairmen are the loneliest guys in town"? The Whirlpool Corp. completed its acquisition on 1 April 2006.

16. It is notable as one of the first companies to produce modern furniture and the manufacturer of the Equa chair, Aeron chair, and Eames Lounge Chair. The company is credited with the invention of the office cubicle (originally known as the "Action Office") under the vision of then-director of research Bob Propst, in 1968. Identify the company.

17. Which company owes its origin to Canadian Lady Corset Company – a small sewing shop in the heart of Montreal founded by Moe Nadler in 1939?

18. Which pen did US Secretary of State James F Byrnes use to sign the paper that brought the United Nations into being in 1945? The brand is owned by the BIC Corporation.

19. Which brand introduced its direct-selling division 'Person to Person' in 2005 and has an independent sales force, known as Comfort Specialist Consultants? They celebrated 2009 as the anniversary year of the introduction of brief.

20. This businesswoman from Bihar has been dubbed the samosa queen from India. She owns a food and catering business serving some of the busiest supermarkets in Britain. Name her.

Answers

1. Lufthansa
2. LiveJournal
3. DHL
4. David Davidar
5. Paramount Pictures
6. Sir Thomas Lipton
7. Lindt
8. Escada
9. Oakley
10. Mr. Potato Head
11. Senheiser
12. Peter Pan
13. Timberland
14. The Phantom of the Opera
15. Maytag Applianes
16. Herman Miller
17. Wonderbra
18. Sheaffer
19. Jockey
20. Parween Warsi

✠✠✠

Potpourri V

Questions

1. Shantilal Parmar spotted Nitin Shah, who worked for a petrol station, and made him a commissioned agent selling jeans. Parmar taught Nitin about the jeanswear business. After this, Nitin envisioned a denim empire and commissioned the help of his brothers Arun and Milan Shah. Identify the denim brand from the above story.

2. Which magazine's title, in French, means "she"? Pierre Lazareff and his wife Hélène Gordon founded the magazine in 1945.

3. Wherever wheels are rolling,
   No matter what the load,
   The name that's known is ....
   Where the rubber meets the road
   Complete the above advertisement jingle that was frequently used in the 1960s and 1970s, especially on televised sporting events.

Maneka Gandhi was first spotted by Sanjay Gandhi in a modeling assignment for Bombay Dyeing.

4. This term was used by the Romans to refer to the Roman province covering much of the island of Great Britain. The name itself derives from Diodorus's rendering of the indigenous name for the Pretani people whom the Greeks believed to inhabit the British Isles. How do we know this term in the world of business?

5. Which winery located in Narayangaon near Pune was started by Mr. Shyamrao Chowgule in 1982?

6. Which brand was promoted with the famous slogan `Put a Tiger in your Tank' that first used it in 1964?

7. Lalji Gala started a bookshop in 1944. In those days selling second-hand books was not common. Lalji Gala saw a business prospect in this and became a pioneer in selling second-hand books in Mumbai.

After some time, he started publishing books also. Which publishing house?

8. What was created in Paris on 21 July 1883 by a group of eminent men, including the scientist Louis Pasteur, the diplomat Ferdinand de Lesseps, the writers Jules Verne and Ernest Renan, and the publisher Armand Colin?

9. Name the band that derives its name from the document issued to people claiming unemployment benefit from the UK government's Department of Health and Social Security (DHSS) at the time of the band's formation.

The original Lifebuoy jingle was sung by Jagjeet Singh – today, one of India's foremost ghazal exponents.

10. Which company makes its products under the brand names – Epiphone, Kramer, Valley Arts, Tobias, Steinberger, and Kalamazoo?

11. Their first book, Across Asia on the Cheap, was written and published by Englishman Tony Wheeler, a former engineer at Chrysler Corp and the University of Warwick and London Business School graduate, and his wife Maureen Wheeler in Sydney in 1973, following a lengthy trip from Turkey, through Iran, Afghanistan and Pakistan, to India or Nepal. Identify.

12. Martin Rapaport's impact within this industry is largely controversial because his commercial price guides have made manipulation of prices much more difficult for the industry, and are considered a step toward commoditizing the industry. Which industry?

13. Name the cosmetics brand owned by L'Oréal that began in 1935, when its founder, Armand Petitjean was exploring the ruins of a castle while vacationing in the French countryside. Petitjean's inspiration for the company's symbol, a golden rose, were the many wild roses growing around the castle.

14. Which company's founder resigned from the Vacuum Oil Company over a disagreement with the management regarding Vacuum Oil's foray into the railroad lubricants sector and set himself up as competitor?

15. Wang Dulu was a Chinese author remembered today mostly for his five-part epic wuxia-romance series, often called collectively the "Crane-Iron Series". Identify the missing title from the list.
    1. Crane Frightens Kunlun
    2. Precious Sword, Golden Hairpin
    3. Sword's Force, Pearl's Shine
    4. ....
    5. Iron Knight, Silver Vase

16. This brand is an all-Australian phenomenon, even though as a company it has been owned by British giant Reckitt & Colman since the late 1960s. It is said that J. Hagemann who invented this brand as an insecticidal powder in the 1870s himself came up with this name, with a little help from his French wife. Which brand?

17. Which company founded in 1761 in Nuremburg is credited with the invention of the pencil?

18. Which private equity firm founded by Peter Peterson and Stephen Schwarzman in 1985 has the name, which is wordplay on the names of the two founders?

19. Which wrigley brand first made during the reign of King George III was sold as the original "curiously strong" mints?

20. In the aftermath of the tsunami in Asia in December 2004, these classic hard red brick shaped bars were a key element in the relief packages distributed in Southern India, Sri Lanka and Indonesia to help prevent the spread of infectious diseases so endemic in the aftermath of such disasters. Identify.

Answers

1. Pepe Jeans
2. Elle
3. Firestone Tire and Rubber Company
4. Britannia
5. Chateau Indage Vineyards
6. Esso
7. Navneet
8. Alliance française
9. UB40
10. Gibson Guitar Corporation
11. Lonely Planet Publications
12. Diamond Industry
13. Lancome
14. Castrol
15. Crouching Tiger, Hidden Dragon
16. Mortein; the famous name is a combination of the French word 'mort' (dead) and the German 'ein' (one).
17. Faber-Castell
18. Blackstone
19. Altoids
20. Lifebuoy Soaps

✠ ✠ ✠

Potpourri VI

Questions

1. The dark blue background of the logo is known to designers as Pantone 294C. Colloquially called the 'Blue Oval', which company's logo is being described?

2. What famous brand of oil, generic to the category of groundnut cooking oil, owned by Ahmed Mills, disappeared from the market following a reported family feud?

3. What famous hotel was founded in 1887 in Singapore and subsequently named after one of the most prominent Westerners who built up the city into the modern country it is today?

Crossword puzzles first appeared in the New York World in 1913, and soon became a popular feature in newspapers. In 1924, Simon's aunt, a crossword puzzle devotee, asked Simon whether there was a book of these puzzles that she could give to a friend. Simon discovered that none had been published, and, with Schuster, launched a company - Simon & Schuster to exploit the opportunity.

4. The logo of which car audio and navigation system manufacturer consists of stripes which stand for excellence in engineer, manufacturing, marketing, service and partner excellence?

5. **Interviewer:** When and why did you decide to become an economist in the first place?

    Interviewee: That's a little embarrassing. I don't know how many of your viewers read science fiction, but there's a very old series by Isaac Asimov – the Foundation novels – in which the social scientists who understand the true dynamics save civilization. That's what I wanted to be; it doesn't exist, but economics is as close as you can get, so as a teenager I really got into it."

    Identify the interviewee.

6. Name the US-based celebrity management company whose annual revenues are estimated to be between $275 and $300 million and had Charlie Chaplin as one of its first clients.

7. Which company calls its customers "Guests", its employees "Team Members", and its supervisors "Team Leaders". Also, managers are known as "Executive Team Lead (ETLs)" and the Store Manager is known as the "Store Team Leader (STL)"? This practice was derived in 1989 from The Walt Disney Company.

Rapper Jay Z is the first non-athlete to get a signature shoe from Reebok.

8. Which designer gained recognition for his design after he was contracted to provide clothing styles for the movie 'The Great Gatsby'?

Wes Cherry created Microsoft Solitaire in 1989 while working as an intern at Microsoft and received no compensation for his popular invention.

9. Miu Miu is positioned as the daily-oriented, younger clothing line from which fashion house that was opened in 1992?

10. Name the classical musicians who run Underscore Records, an initiative that's empowering Indian musicians to share their work with music lovers across the world – on their own terms.

11. The currency of El Salvador coincides with which punctuation mark?

12. International Headquarters of this organization is located at 101 Victoria Street, London. It works in 118 countries. It is called "Sally Ann" in Canada. Identify the organization.

13. Which brand began in 1915 when L.A Jackson founded London Rubber Company?

14. Who was nicknamed "the Crocodile" by fans because of his tenacity on the court?

15. Which US President's wife was the first woman to appear on a US currency note?

IT is the stock symbol for Gartner Inc., the information and technology research and advisory firm headquartered in Stamford, Connecticut.

16. Identify the brand whose label of two horses pulling flagship product of their company is based on Otto von Guericke's experiment with Magdeburg hemispheres.

17. Which product's codename was Kumo, which came from the Japanese word for spider as well as cloud?

Dhara was the first edible oil brand to change from the kilogramme measure to the litre measure in its packaging.

18. Name the US President who had advertised for Phillips Van Heusen in 1953.

19. Arguing against a sought increase in freight rates by Eastern railroads, Louis Brandeis in 1910 cited a theory in court to impress upon the Government that it should not approve the hike as the railroads could save a substantial amount by greater efficiency. This case brought the theory into limelight. Can you name the theory and its proponent?

Dutch Boy paint has been used for some very prestigious jobs including: The Hollywood Sign, The White House, The Golden Gate Bridge, Disney World, US Naval Battleships and aircraft carriers.

20. For Lowe, the advertising agency behind this campaign, the challenge was dealing with a category that had little aspirational value. According to Brand Consultant Harish Bijoor, "This is going beyond the basic requirements of food, clothing and shelter that advertising used to focus on. It has risen above the functional aspect of advertising". Which campaign?

Answers

1. Ford
2. Postman Cooking Oil
3. Raffles
4. Alpine Electronics
5. Paul Krugman
6. William Morris Endeavor Entertainment
7. Target
8. Ralph Lauren
9. Prada
10. Shubha Mudgal and Aneesh Pradhan
11. Colon
12. Salvation Army
13. Durex
14. René Lacoste
15. George Washington
16. Levi's
17. Bing
18. Ronald Reagan
19. Scientific Management – FW Taylor
20. Tata Tea's Jaago Re

✠ ✠ ✠

Potpourri VII

Questions

1. This brand spent $90,000 on advertising in 1906, including $4000 for a page ad in the July issue of the Ladies Home Journal pioneering the use of colour in advertising. The journal ad included a coupon for customers to take to their grocers to sign and return requesting the product and showed company's understanding of push marketing. The company was earlier known as Sanitas Nut Food Co. Which company?

2. The Provisional Government of the French Republic accused the founder of this company of collaborating with Germans and arrested him just after the liberation of Vichy France in 1944. He was incarcerated at Fresnes prison where he died in 1944 under unclear circumstances, awaiting trial. Identify the company.

Spielberg's people approached the makers of M&M's, Mars Inc., with a deal to use the candy in the film - E.T. the Extra-Terrestrial. Notoriously frugal, unpredictable, and tyrannical in their business dealings, chief executives John & Forrest Mars flatly rejected Spielberg's offer. Looking for the best alternative, the movie's producers turned to Hershey Foods for its Reese's Pieces, a relatively new addition to the Hershey product line, which subsequently became very famous.

3. Which department store holding company was formerly Federated Department Stores, Inc?

4. Which city's name means "merchant's harbour" in Danish reflecting its origin as a harbour and a place of commerce.

5. On 1ˢᵗ April 2004, Google ran a hoax for a center that was going to open in 2007. Where exactly would have been this center located?

6. The runners featured in the film 'Chariots of Fire' wore which brand's shoes?

7. In the movie 'The Runaway Bride', as Julia Roberts jumps onto a truck to escape from her marriage, a spectator remarks, "Where's she

going?". Her friend answers "Wherever it is, she will reach by 10 AM." Which company's truck was it?

> *In 1955, Godrej manufactured India's first indigenous typewriter, the market for which was dominated by foreign brands like Remington, Halda and Facit.*

8. Guru Dutt for his film "Kaagaz ke Phool" obtained a copyright licence from 20th Century Fox for what innovation?

9. Five business men set out to mine minerals for grinding wheel abrasives, but finding it as a non-profitable venture, focused on selling sandpaper products. Name the company.

10. Which company was formed by five ex-IBM employees, have an annual function called 'saphire' ?

> *Oracle's flagship product was named "version 2" rather than "version 1" because it believed that customers might hesitate to buy the initial release of its product.*

11. In which movie did the fictional company International Genetic Technologies, Inc. appear for the first time?

12. They come in eight sizes, the largest being a 'Nebuchadnezzar'. What are they?

13. In 1948, a researcher from the Battelle company and an Ohio State University Classics Professor coined a word from Greek origin for a new product. What was the word?

14. Mitchell Kapor, a Bostonian is a teacher of Transcendental Meditation and a Buddhist. In 1988, he started a foundation for electronic free speech. But he is the founder of a well-know company. Identify the Company.

15. This pharmaceutical company's first product (in 1849) was Santonin, which was used to treat intestinal worms. But the bitter taste put off people from consuming it. So, the company came up with the almond toffeeflavoured new Santonin, which was an immediate success. Name the company.

> *Aviva Life Insurance Company India Ltd. is a private insurance company, formed by a joint venture between the Aviva insurance group of UK and the Dabur group of India.*

16. In 1952, Walter Cronkite's coverage of the Democratic and Republican conventions on behalf of CBS led to the coining of a very famous term. Identify is the term.

17. In 1983, a Korean Airlines plane was shot down by the USSR for violating its airspace. The event led to Ronald Reagan releasing which technological facility for civilian use?

18. The company was started by Alexander MacRae under the name of MacRae Hosiery Manufacturers in Bondi Beach, an eastern suburb of Sydney, Australia. Identify.

19. Which consulting major has a social networking platform called "D-Street"?

Subhash Chandra Bose was the CEO of Calcutta Municipal Corporation in 1924.

20. This brand was founded in 1917 by Late Pt. Ram Dayal Joshi. Its registered office is in Kolkata. It publishes a monthly magazine "Sachitra Ayurveda". Which brand?

Answers

1. Kellog's
2. Renault
3. Macy's
4. Copenhagen
5. The Moon
6. Reebok
7. Fedex
8. Cinemascope
9. 3M
10. SAP Lab
11. Jurassic Park
12. Champagne Bottles
13. Xerox from Xerography
14. Lotus
15. Pfizer
16. Anchor
17. Global Positioning System
18. Speedo
19. Deloitte
20. Baidyanath

✠✠✠

Potpourri VIII

Questions

1. July 4, 1939 was a red-letter day for this company, when the Father of the Nation, Mahatma Gandhi, honoured its factory with a visit. He was "delighted to visit this Indian enterprise", he noted later. From the time it came to the aid of the nation gasping for essential medicines during the Second World War, the company has been among the leaders in the pharmaceutical industry in India. Which company?

    The Gunn Report and Showreel of the Year is an annual publication detailing the most successful print and television advertising campaigns of the year. It is authored by Donald Gunn and Emma Wilkie, and published by Flaxman Wilkie. The first report was published in 1999.

2. In 1905, a German immigrant opened a delicatessen store in New York City and started selling mayonnaise using his wife's delicious recipe. In 1912, glass jars with the famous blue ribbons were introduced. Today, the ribbon has become an icon of product quality and proof of the enduring popularity of the mayonnaise. Identify.

    The Singapore Sling is a cocktail that was developed sometime before 1915 by Ngiam Tong Boon, a bartender working at the Long Bar in Raffles Hotel Singapore.

3. In 1865, in the town of Lucca, in the Tuscan heart of Italy's olive growing region, Francesco opened a small storefront business selling regional foods such as olive oil, wine, cheese and olives. From its beginnings in olive oil, this brand has today grown to include a broad range of restaurant-quality pasta sauce and meals. Identify the brand.

4. It was invented in the United States as a medicine by a scientist in 1846 by extracting a healing tea from witch hazel, with which he discovered that he could heal small cuts and other ailments. It became available at many supermarkets across the United States because of its merger with Chesebrough Manufacturing Company in 1955. Identify.

5. Alyque Padamsee recalls shooting with the teenaged Zeenat Aman for this brand of toothpaste. After a difficult shot, Zeenat, who had come from her Panchgani school to Bombay, told him: 'My God, you are a slave-driver.' Identify the toothpaste brand.

6. The name of the person who used it first was Gabrielle. The purpose of making it was to prevent infection of the disease: Syphilis. The name is derived from a word of Latin origin which means a vessel or a container. Identify.

Mumm's label is famous for its red ribbon (Cordon Rouge), patterned after and resembling the French Grand Cordon of the Légion d'Honneur. The company is owned by Pernod Ricard.

7. What was originally made from the personal belongings of the erstwhile rulers of the princely states of Rajputana, Gujarat, the Nizam of Hyderabad and the Viceroy of British India to promote tourism in Rajasthan?

8. What is the word that we use in the world of business whose origin lies in the Roman word for "plunge" or "sink"?

9. It was used by U.S. president Franklin D. Roosevelt in his 7 April 1932 radio address, The Forgotten Man, in which he said, "These unhappy times call for the building of plans that rest upon the forgotten, the unorganized but the indispensable units of economic power...". What did he say should be done with these indispensible units?

The name Typhoo comes from the Chinese word for "doctor". The Typhoo brand is well-known in Britain for its long running television commercial campaign jingle – 'Putting 'T' back into Britain'

10. Which beverage comes from the area near the town of Jerez, Spain and comes in varieties Fino, Manazanilla, Ammontillado and Oloroso?

11. In 1890, an Austrian doctor Robert Gersuny kicked off what by injecting paraffin into women's chests?

In 1951, in the wake of India's 1st General Election, Godrej received an order from Election Commission to manufacture 9 Lac Ballot Boxes at Rs. 44 Lac within 3 months. These ballot boxes were dispatched from the railway sliding at Vikroli to different states.

12. Which faux medical term did the Listerine advertising group create in 1921 to describe bad breath?

13. Which product advertisements used the line ""Always a bridesmaid, never a bride"?

14. Which company traces its roots to the Schwarzchild & Sulzberger company based in New York City that operated meat packing plants? Pepsi Co-owned the company from 1970-85.

15. With its distinctive yellow packaging and bull's head logo, it is one of the oldest existing food brands. In 1866, it was granted the Royal Warrant as manufacturers of mustard to Queen Victoria. Which food brand?

16. Named after a bar in Paris, this American brand of clothing has used Jeffersons stars Isabel Sanford and Sherman Hemsley in a number of its television commercials in the late 1990s. Its co-founder lost his long battle with cancer recently. Identify the brand.

17. Which Italian businessman was the manager of Renault F1 from 2000 to 2009 and was the part-owner and chairman of London's Queens Park Rangers F.C. from 2007 to 2010?

Christian Louboutin's red sole design is the inspiration behind the "Louboutin Manicure" – painting the underside of the nail red and the top black.

18. What was invented by James Watkins, a former engineer for The Pillsbury Company and was originally manufactured by the Golden Valley Microwave Foods?

19. I developed a conceptual model for a perfect company. The primary objective of this company is to make employees as effective as possible. The best products usually come from the most effective employees, so employee effectiveness is the most fundamental of the fundamentals. Who am I?

20. He refined his execution model based on his readings in an economics class about the US Federal Reserve banking system. This is also the reason why he named his company so. Name the company.

Answers

1. Cipla
2. Hellmann's
3. Bertolli
4. Vaseline
5. Signal
6. Condom
7. Palace on Wheels
8. Merger
9. Bottom of the Pyramid
10. Sherry
11. Breast Implants
12. Chronic Halitosis
13. Listerine
14. Wilson sporting Goods
15. Colman's Mustard
16. Old Navy
17. Flavio Briatore
18. Act II Popcorn
19. Scott Adams
20. Fedex

✠✠✠

Section III
Who am I?

Who am I?– Brands & Companies

Question 1

1. I used Led Zeppelin song Rock and Roll and narration by actor Gary Sinise in a commercial for over 3 years.
2. I was formed from the remnants of the Henry Ford Company when Henry Ford departed along with several of his key partners and the company was dissolved.
3. I am named after a French explorer and adventurer who founded the largest city in the state of Michigan.

Question 2

1. As per the historians of advertising, one of my campaigns was considered to be the first in its line to use sex appeal in modern advertising.
2. My cover used to have the picture of a dermatologist on which were blatantly added lines professing my medicinal aura.
3. My lasting tagline has been 'A skin you love to touch'.

Question 3

1. I am the biggest company in the world in my category.
2. My founder was involved in a pro-Nazi movement in the 1940s which he later regretted.
3. My name is formed from the first letters of my founder's name, his family farm and the nearby village to his farm.

Question 4

1. I was started in a bicycle factory and my first product was aircraft engines.
2. My engines were responsible for 29 of the 87 world records for aviation. My next offering was motorbikes and there too I became a world-leader.
3. My lasting line is: 'The Ultimate Driving Machine.'

Question 5

1.   I am the first non-Soviet brand to have signed a former Soviet president as brand ambassador.
2.   Started in 1854, I am the most duplicated brand in the world.
3.   Through the experience with French royalty, my founder developed advanced knowledge of what made a good travelling case.

Question 6

1.   I got evolved from a system called "Camelot".
2.   I have now become a de facto standard for printable documents on the web. I was officially released as an open standard on 1 July 2008.
3.   I am a file format created by Adobe Systems in 1993 for document exchange.

Question 7

1.   My birthplace is Endicott in the USA where I was started with a different name by Herman Hollerith. In 1924, I adopted the name I am known by now.
2.   My employees have won three Nobel prizes, four Turing awards and I am ranked the second largest company in the world in my domain (I was the first ranked till 2006).
3.   My lasting tagline has been: "Business is our middle name".

Question 8

1.   I was incorporated as the Jari corporation in 1949 and got my current name in 1963. In the US and Canada, I now operate as Quixtar.
2.   I have been the centre of several controversies and won a Federal Trade Commission ruling in 1979 that I do not qualify as an illegal pyramid scheme.
3.   My tagline is "Helping people lead better lives."

Question 9

1.   I started life as a wood-pulp mill in 1865 and joined with two other companies, a rubber-works and a cable-works.
2.   I account for nearly one-third of the capitalization of my stock exchange and my revenue exceeds my country's state budget.
3.   My first electronic product was the digital switch. I was named after the town I was formed in which in turn is named after the river that flows through it.

Question 10

1. My founder is the only American to be awarded the Grand Cross of the Golden Eagle, the highest award of the Nazi regime.
2. In 2005, I sold off my wholly-owned subsidiary, Hertz Rent- a-car.
3. My most famous model was called the "Tin Lizzy" and my biggest contribution to the industry is the production process that I introduced.

Question 11

1. The book 'Bug Tales' by Paul Klebahn has 99 hilarious tributes to me.
2. One of the legendary lines about me was "Do you earn too much to afford one?"
3. I was designed at the insistence of one of the more influential people of the 20th century by an engineer who has a brand named after him.

Question 12

1. My founder was brought up by foster parents and started with a small capital and made set-top boxes for TVs.
2. I was so named because my founder had worked on a project of the same name for the CIA.
3. My founder is one of the richest men in the world and his yacht is called "The Rising Sun."

Question 13

1. I am named after the street in London which was the location of my first factory.
2. I started with a product meant for women but ended up becoming famous for celebrating 'masculanity'.
3. My defining ads included Bernstein's theme for the film "The Magnificient Seven."

Question 14

1. My founder's family used to run a bicycle-repair shop in Treviso – and sold his younger brother's bicycle to start his new business in 1955.
2. I am known for my visible and often controversial advertisements.

3. He started by selling sweaters made by my sister to various stores and my own first store was set up in 1968. My less known brands are Sisley, Playlife and Killer Loop.

Question 15

1. I was started by a 17, an 18 and a 19 year old in August 1907 in Seattle. My colour is itself a trademark.
2. I am nick-named 'the big brown machine'.
3. I was started as the American Messenger Company .

Question 16

1. I was founded in 1891 by a maternal cousin of Karl Marx. In 1927, I went on air with a radio station that went off air only during the time the Nazi's invaded my country.
2. My factory was the only industrial facility deliberately bombed by the allied forces during WW2. I introduced the hugely popular compact audio cassette tape in 1963.
3. I shifted my HQ to Amsterdam in 2001. I am the owner of a top football team.

Question 17

1. My corporate philanthropy programme "Live, Learn and Thrive" helps children in need.
2. During the American Civil War, I won contracts to supply the Union Army with soap and candles.
3. I have produced and sponsored the first radio soap operas in the 1930s.

Question 18

1. I started in Kansas, in a shopping and tavern district known as Aggieville.
2. I purchase more than 3 percent of all cheese production in the United States, which requires a herd of about 170,000 dairy cows to produce it.
3. My main advertising slogan is "Gather round the good stuff". On 1 April 2008, I sent emails to customers advertising that I now offer pasta items on my menu which was a publicity stunt held in conjunction with April Fools' Day.

Question 19

1. In 1998, I announced an exclusive licensing agreement with Lucasfilm Ltd. It gave me the right to develop, manufacture and market a new series of products based on themes from the original Star Wars trilogy and the three new Star Wars movies.

2. My motto is "Only the best is good enough", a free translation of the Danish phrase "Kun det bedste er godt nok".

3. My founder was a carpenter from Billund who began making wooden toys in 1932.

Question 20

1. In 1886, my founder abandoned his career as a successful Parisian engineer to take over his grandfather's failing agricultural goods and farm equipment business.

2. My symbol was introduced in 1898, by French artist O'Galop and it is one of the world's oldest trademarks. It has made a brief guest appearance in the Asterix series, as the chariot-wheel dealer in certain translations.

3. I was the owner of the automobile manufacturer Citroën between 1934 and 1976. My first patent was for a removable pneumatic tyre.

Question 21

1. The idea for me was rejected by my founder's professor, but my founder anyway started with his inheritance and some venture capital. The venture started in Little Rock in 1971 and then moved to Memphis Tennessee in 1973

2. I have the largest fleet of aircraft in the world. In Cast Away, Tom Hanks plays an executive in my office

3. I made the following taglines famous:
    i.   Absolutely, positively
    ii. Don't panic
    iii. Whatever it takes

Question 22

1. My founder started by selling matches to neighbours from his bicycle. He found that he could buy matches in bulk very cheaply from

Stockholm and sell them individually at a very low price but still make a good profit. From matches, he expanded to selling fish, Christmas tree decorations, seeds and later ball-point pens and pencils.

2.   My founder was raised on a farm called Elmtaryd, near the small village of Agunnaryd.

3.   'Leading by Design' is a book written by my founder. I had launched a campaign under the slogan, "Just pack up, ship out, find a place of your own. And for all your new things, you know where to come. Make a fresh start".

Question 23

1.   I was developed as an independent project while my creator was working for an American public corporation.

2.   My creator visited Brazil in 2007, in an attempt to understand the success in the country. My name is a slang term for 'Orgasm'. I have been blocked by the Iranian government.

3.   My creator is a Turkish software engineer having earned a Ph.D. in Computer Science from Stanford University.

Question 24

1.   I have used the Beatles song "Revolution" in my 1987 commercial, against the wishes of Apple Records, the Beatles' recording company.

2.   My first professional athlete endorser was Romanian tennis player Ilie Nastase, and my first track endorser was distance running legend Steve Prefontaine. I have also endorsed world's top golf players, including Tiger Woods and Paul Casey.

3.   I initially operated as a distributor for Japanese shoe maker, making most sales at track meets out of my founder's automobile.

Question 25

1.   I ran some TV ads trying to distinguish myself from a similar sounding company. The tag line used in the ads was, "See that blimp up in the sky? We're the other guys!"

2.   I am known for popularising something that was described by Esquire magazine declared as the "Newest Tailoring Idea for Men". Whitcomb Judson is known to be the inventor of this.

3.   In 1946, I invented the tubeless tyre, which was a revolution for the tyre industry.

Answers

1. Cadillac
2. Woodbury Soap
3. IKEA
4. BMW
5. Louis Vuitton
6. PDF format
7. IBM
8. Amway
9. Nokia
10. Ford
11. Volkswagen Beetle
12. Oracle
13. Marlboro
14. United Colors of Benetton
15. United Parcel Services
16. Philips
17. Proctor & Gamble
18. Pizza Hut
19. Lego
20. Michelin
21. Fedex
22. IKEA
23. Orkut
24. Nike
25. Goodrich Corporation

✠ ✠ ✠

Who am I? – People

Question 1

1. On 14 March 1932, I committed suicide with a single gunshot to the heart, leaving a note which read, "My work is done. Why wait?"
2. I had coined the phrase "You Press The Button and We Do The Rest."
3. I am the inventor of a product that formed the basis for the invention of motion picture film, as used by early filmmakers and Thomas Edison.

Question 2

1. My father was a Bengali freedom revolutionary, who having been imprisoned for his political activities, fled Calcutta in the 1920s in order to avoid further prosecution by the British colonial police.
2. To found my company in 1964, for initial capital, I turned to angel investors including my MIT thesis advisor and professor, Dr. Y. W. Lee
3. My company's products are used in GM Cars, Zenith and Phillips TV divisions, NASA space shuttles, the Queen Elizabeth liner, and Broadway theatres.

Question 3

1. I have been toying with the idea of taking up a Hollywood film offer for Noor Jahan, for some time now.
2. My big break came when Mrs. Gandhi got me for the India Festival.
3. I am fond of saying that I sell India's 5000 year old civilization in a jar.

Question 4

1. The patent for the famous mould used for making Toblerone chocolates was given by me.

2. I remain the only United States citizen to be ever offered a position as a foreigner head of state.
3. After graduating, I spent almost two years searching for a teaching post, but a former classmate's father helped me secure a job in Bern, at the Federal Office for Intellectual Property, the patent office, as an assistant examiner.

Question 5

1. In 2006, I became an angel investor for NeoAccel, a network security vendor and maker of SSL VPN-Plus.
2. I am to married Tania Sharma of Nagpur, heiress of the Baidyanath group, in 2008.
3. I began my career at Apple and then joined Firepower Systems Inc.

Question 6

1. I have backpacked around India with a Reed College friend, Daniel Kottke, in search of philosophical enlightenment. I came back with my head shaved and wearing traditional Indian clothing.
2. On 5 December 2007, California Governor Arnold Schwarzenegger and First Lady Maria Shriver inducted me into the California Hall of Fame, located at The California Museum for History, Women and the Arts.
3. I am currently the Walt Disney Company's largest individual shareholder and a member of its Board of Directors.

Question 7

1. I am one of the founders of TiE, The Indus Entrepreneurs.
2. I read about the founding of Intel in Electronic Engineering Times at the age of fourteen and this inspired me to pursue technology as a career.
3. I have invested in an Indian Microfinance NGO, SKS Microfinance, which lends small loans to poor in rural India.

Question 8

1. I was the subject of the piece "Two Young Men Who Went West" in Tom Wolfe's book Hooking Up, a collection of essays and short stories published in 2000.

2. I have been nicknamed "the Mayor of Silicon Valley".
3. I was the co-founder of Fairchild Semiconductor.

Question 9

1. I have served as Economic Advisor to the Government of India.
2. I started my career by hosting "The World This Week" on Doordarshan.
3. My spouse Radhika Roy is the sister of Brinda Karat (CPM politician). Brinda Karat is married to Prakash Karat (General Secretary of CPI(M)).

Question 10

1. I served a jail term quite early in my life but I am known today from my multitude of businesses.
2. I was once called 'Little Tsar' by the Prime Minister of UK.
3. I made a cameo appearance alongside Neha Dhupia in a bollywood film and caused a stir when I turned the actress upside down on a stage.

Question 11

1. In my teens I apprenticed for a hat-maker, but only for a few months, until my father bought the business as a gift for me and my brother.
2. I was sent to India to establish the tax structure, a new paper currency and remodel the finance system of India after the revolt of 1857.
3. In 1843, I established The Economist as a newspaper to campaign for free trade, and acted as Chief editor and sole proprietor for sixteen years.

Question 12

1. My family name derives from the profession of my forefathers, who had been manufacturers of palanquins.
2. Together with my mentor Sir Jamshedji Behramji Kanga, I authored what was then and still is today an authoritative work: The Law and Practice of Income Tax.
3. My famous Annual Budget speeches had humble beginnings in 1958 in a small hall of an old hotel called Green Hotel in Bombay.

Question 13

1. Not so well known, I was in the auditing committee of Mirant's board, a firm that went bankrupt in 2003 after severe liquidity and accounting problems. Mirant was Arthur Andersen's second largest client in the power industry, right after Enron.
2. My parents are Lebanese, I was born in Brazil and educated in France. I have written the book 'Shift'.
3. My life was turned into a comic book series in Japan.

Question 14

1. Born in Piacenza, Italy in 1934, I studied medicine and photography before completing military service.
2. When I returned from service, I took a job as a window dresser in a store named La Rinascente in Milan.
3. I was cemented in the public imagination for dressing Richard Gere in American Gigolo in 1980.

Question 15

1. I was awarded the Presidential Medal of Freedom in March 1992 by President George Bush, Sr., who referred to me as "an American original who epitomizes the American dream ".
2. During World War II, I served as a US Army intelligence officer.
3. I joined JC Penney as a management trainee in Des Moines, Iowa three days after graduating from college.

Question 16

1. I once counted all the broken panes of glass of a factory, publishing in 1857 a "Table of the Relative Frequency of the Causes of Breakage of Plate Glass Windows."
2. I have invented an ophthalmoscope, but the device only came into use after being independently invented by Hermann von Helmholtz
3. I am credited with inventing the first mechanical computer that eventually led to more complex designs.

Question 17

1. My famous euphemism for philandering was 'recharging my batteries'.
2. I am known to have pleaded with President Calvin Coolidge to speak out against speculation, but Coolidge did not listen to me.

3.   Along with Edmund, I created one of the most famous companies in the field of finance till date.

Question 18

1.   I started my career from selling out pickles in the name of 'Priya'.
2.   I am the chairman of Dolphin group of hotels in Andhra Pradesh.
3.   Some of the companies owned by the my group include Margadarsi Chit Fund, Eenadu newspaper, ETV and Ushakiron Movies.

Question 19

1.   I am a qualified Science graduate and was working as a junior chemist in Government laboratory.
2.   The flagship product of my company has been named after my daughter.
3.   A well-known university in Gujarat has been started by me.

Question 20

1.   Growing up, my family lived in the steel making belt of Pennsylvania where my father opened and ran a hot dog restaurant that still stands today – Yocco's.
2.   In 2000, my son-in-law and I launched Olivio Premium Products.
3.   I am known for the revival of Chrysler Corporation.

Question 21

1.   I was the owner of the San Diego Padres baseball team starting in 1974.
2.   I am known for the quote, "The definition of salesmanship is the gentle art of letting the customer have it your way"?
3.   At the age of 52, I invested my entire savings to acquire exclusive distributorship of a milk shake maker – a decision that changed my life.

Question 22

1.   I am currently a lecturer at the Stanford University Graduate School of Business, teaching a course entitled "Strategy and Action in the Information Processing Industry".
2.   I have written over 40 technical papers and hold several patents on

semiconductor devices and technology.

3. Upon graduation, I joined the Research and Development Laboratory of Fairchild Semiconductor and became Assistant Director of Research and Development in 1967.

Question 23

1. I am the author of the book 'Surviving at the Top' written in 1990.
2. I along with National Broadcasting Company (NBC) own 'The Miss Universe Organisation'.
3. I serve as host and executive producer of a NBC reality show.

Question 24

1. I was created by Shigeru Miyamoto and voiced by Charles Martinet since 1995.
2. I first appeared in the 1981 arcade game Donkey Kong as a carpenter named "Jumpman", popularly called "Mr. Video Game" in Japan.
3. I was depicted as a portly plumber who lives in the fictional land of Mushroom Kingdom with Luigi, the younger, taller brother, who is also a plumber.

Question 25

1. I currently head a consulting firm and run a website Trendwatch.
2. I am a regular columnist in The Economic Times and Business World writing about technical analysis.
3. I am famous for coining the term 'Sensex'.

Answers

1. George Eastman; the product was roll film
2. Amar Bose
3. Shahnaz Hussain
4. Albert Einstein
5. Sabeer Bhatia
6. Steve Jobs
7. Vinod Khosla, co-founder of Sun Microsystems
8. Robert Noyce
9. Prannoy Roy
10. Richard Branson
11. James Wilson
12. Nani Palkhivala
13. Carlos Ghosn
14. Giorgio Armani
15. Sam Walton
16. Charles Babbage
17. Charles E. Merrill
18. Ramoji Rao
19. Karsanbhai Patel; founder of Nirma
20. Lee Iacocca
21. Ray Kroc
22. Andy Grove
23. Donald Trump
24. Mario
25. Deepak Mohoni

✠✠✠

Section IV
Picture Perfect

Connect The Dots

Question 1

1

2

3

4

Question 2

1

2

3

4

Question 3

1

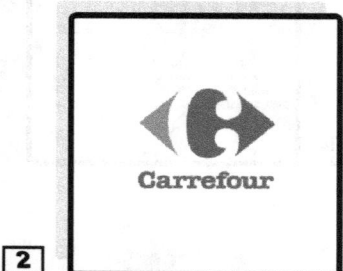

2

3

4

Question 4

1

2

3

4

Question 5

1

2

3

4

Question 6

1

2

Question 7

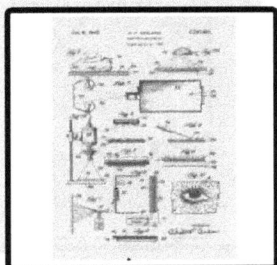

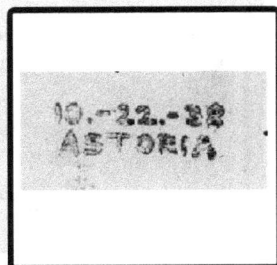

Question 8

1

2

3

4

Question 9

1

2

3

4

Question 10

1

2

3

4

Question 11

1

2

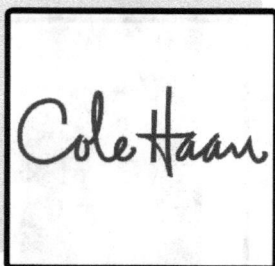

3

4

Question 12

1

2

3

4a

4b

4c

Question 13

1

2

3

4

Question 14

1

2

3

4

Question 15

1

2

3

4

Answers

Answer 1

Pierre Cardin

1.   Pierre Cardin introduced the **bubble dress** in 1954.
2.   Pierre Cardin purchased **Maxim's restaurants** in 1981.
3.   Pierre Cardin was designated **UNESCO** Goodwill Ambassador in 1991.
4.   Pierre Cardin was contacted by **Pakistan International Airlines** to design uniforms for the flag carrier. The uniforms were introduced in 1966 to 1971 and became an instant hit.

Answer 2

Dilip Chhabria

1.   Designed **Aston Martin DB8** for James Bond.
2.   Left job at **GM** to start his own venture.
3.   Designed vanity van for **Shah Rukh Khan**.
4.   Designed the car used in the movie **Tarzan: The Wonder Car** directed by Abbas Mastan.

Answer 3

LVMH Moët Hennessy • Louis Vuitton S.A.

1.   The house of **Givenchy** was founded in 1952 by designer Hubert de Givenchy and is owned by LVMH.
2.   LVMH is one of the shareholders of French retailer **Carrefour**.
3.   In 2001, **De Beers** launched a joint venture with LVMH in order to establish De Beers as a retail brand.
4.   The oldest of the LVMH brands is wine producer **Château d'Yquem**, which dates its origins back to 1593.

Answer 4
Apple Inc.

1.   **George Orwell:** Writer of book something 1984, on which the Apple Macintosh 1984 launch campaign was based.
2.   **Paul Rand:** Designer of Apple Logo.
3.   **Eric Schmidt:** Former member of the board of directors of Apple Inc.
4.   Steve Wozniak was a contestant on ABC's 8th season of **Dancing with the Stars.**

Answer 5
Playboy

1.   The novel **Fahrenheit 451**, by Ray Bradbury, was serialized in the March, April, and May 1954 issues of Playboy magazine.
2.   **Ian Fleming:** The magazine has a long history of publishing short stories by such novelists as Arthur C. Clarke, Ian Fleming, Vladimir Nabokov, and Margaret Atwood.
3.   **Hugh Hefner:** Founder and Chief Creative Officer of Playboy Enterprises.
4.   **Marilyn Monroe:** The first centrefold was Marilyn Monroe, although the picture used originally was taken for a calendar rather than for Playboy.

Answer 6
Ray-Ban

1.   Ray-Ban was introduced for the **United States Army Air Corps.**
2.   Ray-Ban has been partnering the annual **Sundance Film Festival** for independent filmmakers since 2003.
3.   In 1999, Bausch & Lomb sold the brand to the Italian **Luxottica Group**.
4.   Ray-Ban Aviator sunglasses jumped 40%, due to their use by the characters in the film – **Top Gun.**

Answer 7
Xerox

1.   Chester Carlson's **patent** describing "electrophotography," which was issued by the U.S. Patent Office in 1942.
2.   **Chester Carlson** is best known for having invented the process of electrophotography, which produced a dry copy rather than a wet copy, as was produced by the mimeograph process. Carlson's process was subsequently renamed to xerography, a term that literally means "dry writing."
3.   World's first xerographic image.
4.   Xerox sponsors the Factory **Ducati** Team in the World Superbike Championship, under the name of the "Xerox Ducati".

Answer 8
Oprah Winfrey

1.   **The Deep End of the Ocean** by Jacquelyn Mitchard, a bestseller that was the very first novel selected by Oprah Winfrey to be discussed on Oprah's Book Club in 1996.
2.   Winfrey co-founded the women's cable television network **Oxygen**.
3.   **King World Productions, Inc.** was a syndicator of television programming in the United States until its eventual 2007 incorporation into CBS Television Distribution. King World launched Harpo Productions' successful Oprah Winfrey Show in 1984.
4.   In 1985, Winfrey co-starred in Steven Spielberg's epic film adaptation of Alice Walker's Pulitzer Prize-winning novel **The Color Purple**.

Answer 9
RBI

1.   **C D Deshmukh** was the first Indian to be appointed as the Governor of the Reserve Bank of India in 1943 by the British Raj authorities.
2.   **Narayan Murthy** serves as a director on the Central Board of the Reserve Bank of India.
3.   **Ramkinkar Baij** has created the Yaksha and Yakshi sculpture for Reserve Bank of India that stand at its entrance.

4. Yaksha and Yakshini used to guard **Kuber's** gardens and treasures.

Answer 10
HAWKINS

1. Founder – **Dr Vasudeva**
2. Futura by Hawkins is the only pressure cooker in the world to have been displayed by **The Museum of Modern Art**, New York
3. Every Hawkins product carry a **UL label** – a not-for-profit institution testing products for public safety.
4. **Neena Gupta** worked in a Hawkins ad that became quite famous.

Answer 11
NIKE

1 **Nastase** was the first professional sports figure to sign an endorsement contract with Nike in 1972.
2 Nike used the **Beatles** song "Revolution" in a 1987 commercial.
3 Nike's first acquisition was the upscale footwear company **Cole Haan** in 1988.
4 Nike's first self-designed product was based on Bowerman's **waffle** design.

Answer 12
American Express

1. The company's mascot adopted in 1958, is a **Roman gladiator** whose image appears on the company's travelers' cheques and credit cards.
2. American Express was started as an **express mail business** in Albany, New York in 1850.
3. **Stephen King** appeared in American Express ads in 1980s.
4. American Express was founded as a joint stock corporation by the merger of the express companies owned by **Henry Wells** (Wells & Company), **William Fargo** (Livingston, Fargo & Company), and **John Warren Butterfield** (Wells, Butterfield & Company, the successor earlier in 1850 of Butterfield, Wasson & Company).

Answer 13

Twitter

1. Astronaut **Mike Massimino** is the first human to tweet from space
2. **Ashton Kutcher** is the first person or corporation to have one million followers of Twitter.
3. **Mallika Sherawat** visited Twitter headquarters in San Francisco, California in 2009. She is the first Indian star to be invited to visit Twitter headquarters.
4. **Jack Dorsey** – Creator of Twitter

Answer 14

Nintendo

1. In 1966, Nintendo moved into the Japanese toy industry with the **Ultra Hand**, an extendable arm developed by its maintenance engineer Gunpei Yokoi in his free time.
2. Super Mario Bros. is a 1985 platform video game developed by Nintendo, published for the Nintendo Entertainment System as a sequel to the 1983 game **Mario Bros.**
3. Founded by Fusajiro Yamauchi, Nintendo produced handmade **hanafuda** cards as their first product.
4. Nintendo of America is the majority owner of the **Seattle Mariners** Major League Baseball team.

Answer 15

Punjab National Bank

1. **Sardar Dyal Singh Majithia** was the Chairman, Board of Directors of the Punjab National Bank.
2. **Lala Lajpat Rai** was actively associated with the management of the Bank in its early years.
3. PNB has had the privilege of maintaining accounts of national leaders such as Mahatma Gandhi, Shri Jawahar Lal Nehru, Shri Lal Bahadur Shastri, Shrimati Indira Gandhi, as well as the account of the famous **Jalianwala Bagh** Committee.
4. **R K Dalmia**: Dalmia Group acquired controlling interests in the Punjab National Bank and in the Times of India group of publications during 1940s.

For Your Eyes Only

1. Identify the French fashion designer.

2. Life and Debt, a documentary film, deals with which institution's policies' influence on Jamaica and its economy from a critical point of view?

3. Identify him.

4. Whose statue?

5. Which company was started by him?

6. Which business empire's heir created this film?

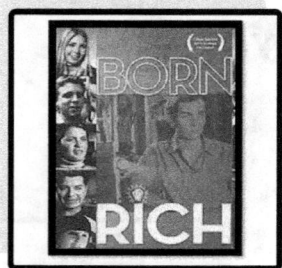

7. Who was the first editor of Trump, published by Hugh Hefner in 1957?

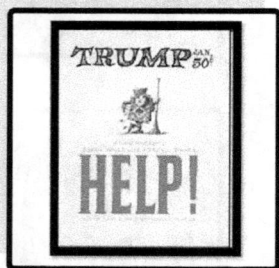

8. He is known as the father of modern advertising. Who is he?

9. New joinees of which company are required to wear these colourful caps for the initial few weeks? What name is given to them?

10. Identify the marketing guru who inspired us to broaden our vision.

11. Which institution's logo?

12. Which company was founded by the person shown in the picture?

14. Identify the brothers.

13. Identify the service by Google.

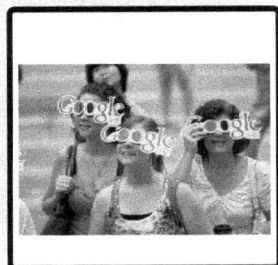

15. An ad for which world famous brand?

Let your fingers do the walking!

Answers

1. Yves Saint Laurent
2. IMF
3. Eric Morley, founder of the Miss World pageant
4. Arthur Brooke
5. Paramount Airways
6. Johnson & Johnson
7. Harvey Kurtzman, founding editor of MAD magazine
8. Albert Lasker
9. Google and Nooglers
10. Theodore Levitt
11. ISCKON
12. Penguin Books. The guy in the picture is the founder of the company–Allen Lane.
13. Google Goggles. Google Goggles lets you use pictures taken with your mobile phone to search the web.
14. Warner Brothers
15. Yellow Pages

✠✠✠

Section V
Questions

All about Reports: Consulting

Questions

1. Which company played key roles in the development of operations research, the word processor, the first synthetic penicillin, LexisNexis, and NASDAQ? Today the company is one of the world's leading management consulting firms, working closely with Fortune 500 firms across the globe.

    > *The first management consulting firm was Arthur D. Little, founded in 1886 by the MIT professor of the same name.*

2. What was founded by Serge Kampf in 1967 as an enterprise management and data processing company as the Société pour la Gestion des Enterprises et le Traitement de l'Information (Sogeti)?

3. Which consulting company was established in 1973 by seven former partners from the Boston Consulting Group? The company pioneered the approach of aligning its incentives with its clients' results and occasionally taking equity in lieu of fees. The firm took an ownership stake in fruit processor Del Monte Foods while working to revamp the company's strategy.

    > *Zulfiqar Ali Bhutto – President and Prime Minister of Pakistan.*
    > *Karan Bilimoria – Founder of Cobra Beer.*
    > *Both of them have been former employees of Ernst & Young.*

4. The acronym 'MBB' stands for which top three pure strategy consulting firms?

5. It began as a branch of McKinsey & Company. In 2006, it completed management buyout from EDS and became an independent, privately owned firm. Identify the firm.

6. Name the privately-owned global management consulting firm that

was founded in 1983 by a group of six entrepreneurs with ties to the Harvard Business School: Michael Porter, Mark Fuller, Joseph Fuller, Michael Bell, Mark Thomas, and Thomas Craig.

7. The founder of this company was the first person to be appointed an independent auditor of a public company. In 1993, the international firm was renamed to reflect the contribution from the Japanese firm. Which company?

8. A former Bible salesman, Bruce D. Henderson left HBS ninety days before graduation to work for Westinghouse Corporation, where he became one of the youngest vice presidents in the company's history. He left Westinghouse to head Arthur D. Little's management services unit before accepting an improbable challenge from the CEO of the Boston Safe Deposit and Trust Company to start a consulting arm for the bank. Which company did he start?

9. Which company was notoriously known as "CIA of Wall Street" in 1980's?

10. This company was the official worldwide information technology partner of the Olympic Games, having provided and run all IT infrastructure for the Olympic Games in Beijing 2008. It acquired KPMG Consulting in the United Kingdom and in the Netherlands in 2002. The company logo is a surgeonfish; the powder blue tang. Which company?

Answers

1. Arthur D. Little
2. Capgemini
3. Bain & Company
4. McKinsey, BCG, Bain
5. A.T. Kearney
6. Monitor Group
7. Deloitte
8. Boston Consulting Group
9. Kroll Associates
10. Atos Origin

✠✠✠

Apparel Companies

Questions

1. My founder's first name is derived from the Hebrew word meaning 'joining', 'attached' or 'adhesion'. He was a German merchant living in San Francisco, California. One of my frequent customers was a tailor by the name of Jacob Davis. Who am I?

2. Spain's richest man Amancio Ortega Gaona is the founder of which fashion group? Zara that was described by CNN as a "Spanish success story" is the flagship chain store of this group.

3. Identify the US-based clothing stores founded by Mel and Patricia Ziegler in 1978 as a travel-themed clothing company that was bought by Gap in 1983.

Founded in 1973 by Gordon and Rena Merchant, the name billabong came from the same word, which is a stagnant body of water attached to a waterway.

4. Which American clothing and accessories retailer took part in the Product Red campaign releasing a special RED collection, including a T-shirt manufactured in Lesotho from African cotton in spring 2006? Old Navy, Forth & Towne and Piperlime are the brands that are owned by this retailer.

5. Which company was established first as Reading Glove and Mitten Manufacturing Company in Pennsylvania in October of 1899 by John Barbey and a group of investors?

6. Which brand's name coincides with the title that was given to a student obtaining first class in the Cambridge Mathematics Tripos I examination? Their 13MWZ style, introduced in 1947, is still available worldwide.

7. Which Kansas-based company founded National Denim Day as part of National Breast Cancer Awareness Month in 1996?

8. He is a stylish young man wearing a shirt with the detached collar.

By 1920, he used to receive more than 17 thousand fan letters a day, more than many of the popular film stars. President Theodore Roosevelt referred to him as a "superb portrait of the common man". He inspired a Broadway musical Helen of Troy in 1923. Who?

☀ The song "Heart and Soul" by T'Pau was used to advertise Pepe Jeans in 1987.

9. In 1881, Moses and his wife Endel began sewing shirts by hand and selling them from pushcarts to local anthracite coal miners. The small business started by the two is now a big company. The company received a patent for a self-folding collar in 1919, which was released to the public in 1921. Which company?

10. Which brand, launched in 1993, was responsible for popularizing the phrase "Friday dressing"?

Answers

1. Levis
2. Inditex
3. Banana Republic
4. Gap
5. VF Corp
6. Wrangler Jeans
7. Lee
8. The Arrow Collar Man
9. Phillips-Van Heusen
10. Allen Solly

✠✠✠

Celebrities in Business

Questions

1. Who owns "The Playtone Company" – an American film and television Production Company? It was named after the fictional record company "Playtone" in That Thing You Do!

2. Who founded Hyde Park Entertainment in 1999-one of the leading independent entertainment companies in Hollywood today? It has produced over 100 films, including Jeans and Hollywood fils such as Antitrust, Walking Tall, and Bringing Down the House.

> *Plan B Entertainment is a film production company founded by Brad Pitt, Brad Grey, and Jennifer Aniston. Pitt became the sole owner of the company in 2006.*

3. With whom can you associate Curious Perfume launched in 2004 that represents the young woman that pushes boundaries and revels in adventure?

4. Who joined forces with Andy Hilfiger in April 2001 to form the JLO brand holding company, Sweetface Fashion Company? Under the Sweetface umbrella, they have created a complete lifestyle brand with 11 different product categories.

5. Which American actor, film producer and rapper started the American entertainment company 'Overbrook Entertainment' based in Beverly Hills, California, USA ? The name "Overbrook" is derived from actor's high school in West Philadelphia, Overbrook High School.

> *One Race Films is a video production company established in 1995 in Los Angeles by actor, writer, director, and producer-Vin Diesel.*

6. Who designed a clothing line, DB07, for Marks & Spencers?

7. "I would have been a biscuit maker," he said, when asked in an interview what he would have been had it not been for his current

job! Biscuit manufacturing would not have been a problem for him, as his father has been running Luckyland Biscuits for the past three decades, and it now is the third-biggest biscuit maker in Sri Lanka. Name him.

8. Name the theme restaurant chain inspired by the popular portrayal of Hollywood and was launched in New York on 22 October 1991, with the backing of Hollywood stars Sylvester Stallone, Bruce Willis, Demi Moore, and Arnold Schwarzenegger?

9. Which novelist states on her website, "Creating the fragrance was very much a team effort, blending the inspiration of many people, how they perceive me and how I perceive both my readers and the world I try to create with my books."?

10. MatchCast & Scorite (for cricket) and TenAce (for tennis) are the products of which company?

Answers

1. Actor Tom Hanks and producer Gary Goetzman
2. Ashok Amritraj
3. Britney Spears
4. Jennifer Lopez
5. Will Smith
6. David Beckham
7. Muttiah Muralidharan
8. Planet Hollywood
9. Danielle Steel
10. Stump Vision by Anil Kumble

✠ ✠ ✠

Fountainhead: Origin of Terms

Questions

1. This Japanese word is usually translated as "divine wind". The word originated as the name of major typhoons in 1274 and 1281, which dispersed Mongolian invasions fleets. Which word?

2. This word comes from the Latin word for 'to turn', because of its original connotation of turning attention or drawing attention to something. Identify the word.

The word 'Loophole' comes from a term for an opening in a wall, which was used to shoot arrows from within a building. It is now present in English in the figurative sense of 'outlet, or means of escape', mainly in legal contexts.

3. This term was coined by Hywell Murell in UK in 1949 and was used for study of interaction of technology they use and environment they work in. Identify the term.

4. Which word owes its origin to a French word 'bougette' meaning 'purse'?

5. The credit for popularizing which term may be given to Arnold Toynbee, whose lectures given in 1881 gave a detailed account of the process?

6. Greek slave traders often bartered salt for slaves, giving rise to the expression that someone was "not worth his salt". This describes the origin of which word?

7. This term originally comes from 'spiced ham' and referred to the surplus quantities of 'spiced ham' that were circulated in England during World War II. Now, because this was bland and tasteless nobody really wanted it, yet people were forced to buy it because the Government was diverting all other food to the war effort, due to which it was parodied by Monty Python. Many years later, this term got its present meaning in another field. Which term?

8. Which word originates from the Latin word, which means "to lay open" and more directly as a shortened version of the term which originally denoted an open for public reading royal decree granting exclusive rights to a person?

> *The word franchisee originally came from the French, meaning to be "free from servitude." Franchising dates back to at least the 1850s; Isaac Singer, who made improvements to an existing model of a sewing machine, wanted to increase the distribution of his sewing machines.*

9. From the Latin word for "to weigh", which term is used for a fixed payment or salary, particularly that of a clergyman?

10. Name the Latin expression that refers to a written account of one's past history and is loosely transalated as 'Course of Life' in latin.

Answers

1. Kamikaze
2. Advertise
3. Ergonomics
4. Budget
5. Industrial Revolution
6. Salary
7. Spam
8. Patent
9. Stipend
10. Curriculum Vitae

✠ ✠ ✠

High Street Fashion

Questions

1. This Italian fashion house began in 1918 when Adele Casagrande opened a leather and fur shop in Via del Plebiscito in central Rome. It is best known for its "baguette" handbags. Which fashion house?

2. This label, named after its founder's surname, was founded in 1913. The founder established two boutiques in Milan, and designed and sold handbags, shoes, trunks and suitcases. In the 1990s, it acquired shares in the company Fendi. In May 2007, it joined forces with cell phone maker LG Electronics to create a cell phone. Identify the label.

3. In 1946, this French designer was able to open his own fashion house, backed by textile manufacturer Marcel Boussac. For his first collection in 1947, he created what became immensely famous as the "New Look", which featured rounded shoulders, a cinched waist and a very full skirt. Who?

> ☀ *Coco Chanel took on the nickname "Coco" after her 1905 performance of the song, "Qui qu'a vu Coco dans le Trocadero" for a crowd of uniformed admirers at La Rotande, a music hall in a small, provincial town.*

4. This Algerian-born French fashion designer left home at the age of 17 to work for Christian Dior. Following the latter's death in 1957, the former, at the age of 21, was put in charge of the effort of saving the fashion house from financial ruin. He created the famous classic tuxedo suit for women in 1966—Le Smoking suit. Who?

5. She was a cabaret singer before she became famous in the world of fashion. Though her first name was Gabrielle, she is known by her nickname. She launched a legendary perfume named after her in 1921, and also the "little black dress" in 1926. Identify the designer.

6. This designer founded the company named after him in Florence in 1906 as a leather saddlery shop. Soon the company became famous for leather bags for horsemen, and expanded its business to Rome

and subsequently to Milan and Manhattan. Guinness World Records cites this designer's "Genius Jeans" as the most expensive jeans in the world. This company now belongs to French conglomerate company Pinault-Printemps-Redoute (PPR). Which designer?

Gabardine – a hardwearing, water-resistant yet breathable fabric, in which the yarn is waterproofed before weaving was invented by Thomas Burberry in 1880.

7. This Italian designer originally trained in medicine before becoming a photographer. He then was in the army, and subsequently worked in a department store. He then worked as a designer, and in 1974, he established a menswear label along with his partner. Who?

8. This Italian privately held fashion house was created by a duo, one born in Sicily, and the other in Milan. They started their own business in 1982 but were officially on the map of fashion after participating in the Milano Collezioni's "New Talents" fashion show. Identify the duo.

9. Commonly referred to as the "Zucca" print in its original form and "Zucchino" in its smaller style, this fashion house's iconic "double F" logo pattern was first designed by Karl Lagerfeld in the 1960s. Identify the fashion house.

Kanye West once appeared at a party with the logo of Fendi shaved into his head.

10. Prior to starting the label, the founder used to work for Brooks Brothers. In 1968, he started a line of men's ties. By 1969, he had a boutique store within the Manhattan department store Bloomingdale's. Identify the label.

Answers

1. Fendi
2. Prada
3. Christian Dior
4. Yves Saint Laurent
5. Coco Chanel
6. Guccio Gucci
7. Giorgio Armani
8. Dolce & Gabbana
9. Fendi
10. Ralph Lauren

✠✠✠

It's all about Money

Questions

1. This four-letter Botswana currency, which replaced rand in 1976, means 'rain' in the local language. It has the ISO 4217 code BWP and is subdivided into 100 thebe. What's the name of the currency?

2. Hyrule is a common fictional kingdom appearing in the Legend of Zelda video game series. The currency in this kingdom, apart from being used to purchase stuff, has other uses. These include ability to use arrows, ability to summon a fairy to increase the arsenal, powering the magical armour, etc. What is the name of currency?

How "buck" became slang for U. S. dollar?
The term originated from the Old West when buckskin was a common medium of exchange with Indians. Later as currency replaced the barter system, people still refer to a dollar as a buck (short for buckskin).

3. All the Mughal emperors who ruled in India used silver coins that were introduced by Sher Shah Suri. What were these silver coins called?

4. What was declared the national motto of the United States by the 84th U.S. Congress and was first used on paper money in 1957, when it appeared on the One Dollar Silver Certificates?

5. Which was the first mint in the country to mint coins of stainless steel?

6. Currency of which country means "marten" since it is based on the use of marten pelts as units of value in medieval trading?

People used to save their cash in kitchen jars made of a clay called pygg and called them pygg jars. Later they became known as piggy banks and were made in the shape of pigs.

7. What is a coin with a minting error called?

8. Who took up the post of Warden of the Mint, responsible for investigating cases of counterfeiting, in 1696, and subsequently held the office of Master of the Royal Mint from 1699 until his death in 1727?

Rand takes its name from the Witwatersrand, the ridge upon which Johannesburg is built and where most of South Africa's gold deposits were found.

9. Name the internal currency of Second Life that can be used to buy, sell, rent or trade land or goods and services with other users.

10. What is meant by 'Trial of the Pyx'?

Answers

1. Pula
2. Rupee
3. Rupiya
4. In God We Trust
5. The NOIDA mint
6. Croatia (Kuna)
7. FIDO. In coin collecting term, FIDO = Freaks, Irregulars, Defects, Oddities.
8. Sir Isaac Newton
9. Linden dollar (L$)
10. The Trial of the Pyx is the procedure in the United Kingdom for ensuring that newly-minted coins conform to required standards.

    The term "Pyx" refers to the boxwood chest in which coins were placed for presentation to the jury. There is also a Pyx Chapel (or Pyx Chamber) in Westminster Abbey, which was once used for secure storage of the Pyx and related articles.

✠ ✠ ✠

Management Gurus

Questions

1. Who established in 1990 "Leader to Leader Institute" for non-profit Management, the Leader to Leader Institute furthers its mission–to strengthen the leadership of the social sector–by providing social sector leaders with essential leadership wisdom, inspiration and resources to lead for innovation and to build vibrant social sector organizations?

   Gary Hamel is the originator (with C. K. Prahalad) of the concept of core competencies. He is also the director of the Woodside Institute, a non-profit research foundation based in Woodside, California.

2. Which Harvard Business School professor has coined terms such as 'undershoot' and 'overshoot' with respect to valuations of products in the IT industry?

3. He explains Synergy as 2+2=5, or how the whole is greater than the mere sum of the parts, and it requires an examination of how opportunities fit the core capabilities of the organisation. His book was the first text to concentrate entirely on strategy in 1960's. Identify the management guru.

   C.K. Prahalad, praising their supply chain, described Mumbai Dabbawallahs as a "model of managerial and organisational simplicity."

4. Fill in the blanks: In 1981, management guru Peter Drucker said that the best-run organization in the US was ....?

5. Whose business card reads 'onward, forward, upward, ...'.

6. Which famous management thinker propounded the concept of Theory X and Theory Y management styles in his famous book 'The Human Side of Enterprise'?

7. Whose claim?

   "Most of the work being done does not add any value for customers, and this work should be removed, not accelerated through automation. Instead, companies should reconsider their processes in order to maximize customer value, while minimizing the consumption of resources required for delivering their product or service."

8. He partnered with Kevin Cope and Stephen M.R. Covey to form Acumen Learning. He has helped to define and popularize the idea of business acumen being an essential leadership characteristic in management. Identify him.

Peter Drucker's first major book was The End of Economic Man: The Origins of Totalitarianism (1939), and last book was The Effective Executive in Action (published in January 2006).

9. 'Reengineering the Corporation' was ranked among the "three most important business books of the past 20 years" by Forbes magazine. Identify the famous author of the book.

10. Name the American management expert who co-founded Strategos, an international management consulting firm based in Chicago.

Answers

1.   Peter Drucker
2.   Clayton Christensen
3.   Igor Ansoff
4.   The Girl Scouts of America
5.   Edward De Bono
6.   Douglas McGregor
7.   Michael Porter
8.   Ram Charan
9.   Michael Hammer
10. Gary Hamel

✠ ✠ ✠

Newsmakers for Wrong Reasons

Questions

1. Which company began in Mississippi in 1983 as Long Distance Discount Services Inc.? Beginning in 1999 and continuing through May 2002, the company used fraudulent accounting methods to mask its declining earnings by painting a false picture of financial growth and profitability to prop up the price of its stock.

    The scandal by Salomon trader Paul Mozer who was caught submitting false bids to the U.S. Treasury by Deputy Assistant Secretary Mike Basham, in an attempt to purchase more Treasury bonds than permitted by one buyer between December 1990 and May 1991 is covered extensively in the 1993 book "Nightmare on Wall Street".

2. Who is the author of the book 'Back from the Brink: Coping with Stress' released in June, 2005?

3. Name the CEO of WorldCom (now MCI Inc.) who was found guilty of all charges and convicted of fraud, conspiracy and filing false documents with regulators — all related to the $11 billion accounting scandal at the telecommunications company he founded.

4. Founded in 1961 by Calisto Tanzi, this company collapsed in 2003 with a $20 billion hole in its accounts in what remains Europe's biggest bankruptcy. Since 2011, it is a subsidiary of French group Lactalis. Identify the company.

    The top bond traders at Salomon Brothers called themselves "Big Swinging Dicks", and were the inspiration for the books "The Bonfire of the Vanities" and "Liar's Poker".

5. Fortune named it "America's Most Innovative Company" for six consecutive years. This firm claimed revenues of $111 billion in

2000. At the end of 2001 it was revealed that its reported financial condition was sustained mostly by institutionalized, systematic and creatively planned accounting fraud. Which company?

6. This English company was granted a monopoly to trade with South America under a treaty with Spain. The government and the company convinced the holders of around £10 million of short-term government debt to exchange it with a new issue of stock in the company. Rumours of possible profits led to overheated speculation in this company's shares. However, when the voyages were delayed and little actual profit resulted, the share price collapsed. Identify the company.

7. Whom did the journalist Sucheta Dalal in a column in *The Times of India* expose on April 23, 1992?

Rogue Trader is a 1999 drama film directed by James Dearden about former derivatives broker Nick Leeson and the 1995 collapse of Barings Bank.

8. Name the former CEO and chairman of CA Inc. who received a 12-year prison sentence for orchestrating the scandal.

9. He is a former derivatives trader whose unsupervised and unauthorized speculative trading on Singapore International Monetary Exchange (SIMEX) caused the spectacular collapse of Barings Bank. Who is he?

10. Which financial institution of Dutch origin purchased Barings Bank in 1995 for the nominal sum of £1 and sold the U.S.-based operations to ABN Amro for $275 million in 2001?

Answers

1. WorldCom (now MCI Inc.)
2. Nick Leeson
3 Bernard Ebbers
4. Parmalat
5. Enron
6. South Sea Company
7. Harshad Mehta
8. Sanjay Kumar
9. Nick Leeson
10. ING

✠✠✠

Retail Revolution

Questions

1. In 1940, during a visit to a store in Des Moines, Iowa, who trained a young Sam Walton on how to wrap packages with a minimal amount of ribbon?
2. Which retailing company traces its origins to a six-storey building constructed by George Dayton in downtown Minneapolis in 1901?
3. The origin of which supermarket chain can be traced back to Muthusamy Mudaliar, who was a mail runner for the British in colonial India?

The Body Shop created a doll in the likeness of Barbie with the name Ruby but with a lifelike voluptuous figure and luxuriant red hair, that came with the tag line, "There are 3 billion women who don't look like supermodels and only 8 who do".

4. The first store of which hypermarket chain was opened in 1957 in France near a crossroads?
5. Name the food retailer whose original name was formed from the Dutch phrase literally meaning "through united co-operation everyone regularly profits".

Wal-Mart operates in Mexico as Walmex, in the United Kingdom as Asda, in Japan as Seiyu, and in India as Best Price.

6. Name the diversified German retail group that was established in 1964 by Otto Beisheim.
7. Odyssey is a retail format for books from which Indian conglomerate?
8. Who started his first business as a Draper, at 228, Borough High Street, Southwark, London?
9. Which business started as a small car radio installation in 1968 in a small rented space below a car park in Sydney?
10. My founder is believed to have coined the phrase "the customer is always right". Who am I?

Answers

1.   James Cash Penny
2.   Target Corporation
3.   Nilgiris
4.   Carrefour
5.   Spar
6.   Metro
7.   Deccan Chronicle
8.   Charles Henry Harrod
9.   Dick Smith
10. Selfridges

✠✠✠

Sports Goods Manufacturers

Questions

1. The first word of the name of this manufacturer means "without equal" in French. Identify the manufacturer.
2. Which company was founded in 1876 by a pitcher and the manager of a baseball team in Chicago?

   ⁂ A Wilson volleyball "co-starred" alongside Tom Hanks in the film Cast Away (2000), the volleyball was called Wilson.

3. This company was the result of a merger of two firms in 1940. One of the firms was founded in Cambridge by a world racquets champion in 1855. Its endorsers include former England captains Mike Atherton and Nasser Hussain. Which company?

   ⁂ Gray-Nicolls was the first cricket company to use coloured bat labels.

4. This company is an American importer and manufacturer of inexpensive mass-market bicycles and golf equipment. It was founded in 1887 when the founder purchased the Davis Sewing Machine Company and moved its factory to Ohio. It manufactures sporting goods, including the Hydra-Rib basketball systems used by the NBA. Which company?
5. This Australian company shares its name with a bird. It was founded in 1890 as A.G. Thompson Pty Ltd by Alfred Grace Thompson, a migrant harness and saddle maker who turned to manufacturing the current product line when his livelihood was threatened by the advent of the motor car. Which company?
6. When he passed away on 5 June 2001, Forbes described him as the largest maker of golf clubs in the world. The eponymous company he built uses his first name as its NYSE ticker symbol. Identify.
7. Which company traces its roots to the Schwarzchild & Sulzberger company based in New York City that operated meat packing plants?

8. The company was founded in 1946 by Minoru Yoneyama as a producer of wooden floats for fishing nets. The company was later forced out of this market because of the invention of plastic floats. Which company?

9. Which company was appointed as the official tennis ball supplier to Wimbledon in 1902 and with the current deal set to run until 2015, it remains one of the longest unbroken sporting sponsorships in history?

Russell Corporation is a wholly owned subsidiary of Berkshire Hathaway. Russell markets its products under many brands and subsidiaries, including Russell Athletic, Spalding, Huffy, and Brooks.

10. The company was founded in 1910 in Cheshire as Humphreys Brothers Clothing. In 1924, the company changed its name to the present name, a contraction of its previous name. Which company?

Answers

1. Sanspareil Greenlands, or SG
2. Spalding
3. Gray-Nicolls
4. The Huffy Corporation
5. Kookaburra Sport
6. Ely Callaway (Callaway Golf Co.)
7. Wilson Sporting Goods
8. Yonex
9. Slazenger
10. Umbro

✠✠✠

Textiles and Apparels

Questions

1. This is a type of sweater/jumper that ties, buttons or zips down the front. It is named after James Thomas Brudenell who commanded the charge of the Light Brigade during the Crimean war. What article of clothing is this?

2. What was designed by Jaques Heim and originally called the Atome? It is named after an atoll in Marshall Islands, the site of many American Nuclear Tests.

Haute couture is the french word for "high sewing" or "high dressmaking". It refers to the creation of exclusive custom-fitted clothing. It originally referred to Englishman Charles Frederick Worth's work, produced in Paris in the mid-nineteenth century.

3. What garment does a young Malcolm X described as: "A killer-diller coat with a drape shape, reet pleats and shoulders padded like a lunatic's cell." They first gained popularity in Harlem Jazz culture in the late 1930s, where they were initially called drapes.

During the Crimean War, knitted balaclava helmets were sent over to the British troops to help protect them from the bitter cold weather. The name "balaclava" comes from the town of Balaklava, near Sevastopol in Ukraine.

4. BASF was founded in Germany, by Friedrich Engelhorn in 1865 for the production of dyes. In 1867, research into synthesis of the dye indigo was successfully concluded. What was the effect of the research?

5. They were a fad in the United States during the 1920s, particularly with (male) college students in the mid- and later years of the decade. They are full-length fur coats. They became popular due to the stories of Davy Crockett and popular artist James Van Der Zee. What are we talking about?

6. What type of headgear is named after the third largest city in Morocco?

7. Emilio Pucci made the first designer version of this costume. He was inspired by the baggy pants cut off at the ankle worn by fishermen at a popular European summer resort. The item became really popular after Audrey Hepburn was seen sporting them in Roman Holiday. Identify.

8. This word is derived from the name of a French material, serge de Nimes: serge (a kind of material) from Nimes (a town in France). Identify the word.

9. This is a type of sleeve whose distinguishing characteristic is to extend in one piece fully to the collar, leaving a diagonal seam from armpit to collarbone. It is named after Fitzroy Somerset who served as a General during the Crimean war. It is believed that this sleeve was designed for him to fit his coat when he lost his arm in the Battle of Waterloo. Which article of clothing is it?

10. This is a traditional flat cap worn in Sicily that is made of tweed. Its name is believed to be the Sicilian adaptation of the word 'cap'. The name of the cap is best known to us because it is also the surname of a famous movie director. Identify?

Answers

1. Cardigan
2. Bikini
3. Zoot suit
4. Jeans became affordable
5. Raccoon Coats
6. Fez
7. Capri
8. Denim
9. Raglan sleeve
10. Coppola

✠✠✠

Thank you for Smoking

Questions

1. Which brand of cigarette advertised that their cigarette was "a silly millimeter longer"? A royal warrant was issued to the British company in 1878, after the required five years of supply to the royal family. It was revoked in 1999 due to a "lack of demand in the royal households"

2. Which brand of cigarette was advertised as "just what the doctor ordered"?

   The journey of Cohiba began when Fidel Castro noticed that his bodyguard often smoked a "very aromatic, very nice" cigar. When asked by Castro what brand he smoked, he replied that it was rolled by a friend of his working at the La Corona factory in Havana named Eduardo Rivera. Thus began Cohiba's journey and it became a private brand supplied exclusively to Fidel Castro and high-level officials in the Communist Party of Cuba and Cuban government.

3. In late 1987, RJR created a mascot for a brand about which the American Medical Association published a report stating kids could more easily recognize him than Mickey Mouse, Fred Flintstone, Bugs Bunny or even Barbie. Identify the mascot.

4. Which word comes from a Marwari word for a leaf wrapped in betel nuts, herbs, and condiments?

5. Which brand of cigarette was advertised as "The first truly feminine cigarette—almost as pretty as you are"? They were introduced in 1971 as competition for rival Philip Morris corporation's Virginia Slims.

6. The motto beneath the coat of arms on the cigarette package of this brand is "veni vidi vici" (I came, I saw, I conquered). Richmond, Virginia is now the location of the largest cigarette manufacturing plant of the brand. Which brand?

King Edward VII enjoyed smoking cigarettes and cigars, much to the chagrin of his mother, Queen Victoria. After her death, legend has it, King Edward said to his male guests at the end of a dinner party, "Gentlemen, you may smoke." In his name, a line of inexpensive American cigars has long been named King Edward.

7. Which company holds the license for Davidoff perfumes that includes Cool Water?

8. In 1917, the brand started using the slogan "It's Toasted" to inform the consumers about the manufacturing method in which the tobacco is toasted rather than sun-dried. The message "L.S.M.F.T." was introduced on the package in the same year. It is owned by the American Tobacco Company (ATC). Identify the brand.

9. Identify the brand of cigars whose logo consists of a triangle of six swords surrounding a fleur-de-lis, that was designed by John Hunter Morris and Elkan Co. Ltd., the brand's British distributor.

A popular legend holds that the favorite cigar of US President John F. Kennedy was the H. Upmann Petit Coronas, and that the night before the embargo was signed, he had aide Pierre Salinger procure every box he could gather from Washington, DC tobacconists, for a total of 1,200 of his favourite cigars.

10. In a series of advertisements made many years before he took office, former US President Ronald Reagan was a spokesman for this brand of cigarette. In one of them he is seen addressing cartons of cigarettes as Christmas gifts for "all my friends". Identify.

Answers

1. Benson & Hedges
2. L & M cigarettes
3. Joe Camel
4. Beedi
5. Marlboro
6. Eve
7. Coty
8. Lucky Strike; the message "L.S.M.F.T." stands for "Lucky Strike means fine tobacco".
9. Montecristo
10. Chesterfield

✠✠✠

Section VI
Crosswords

Crossword 1

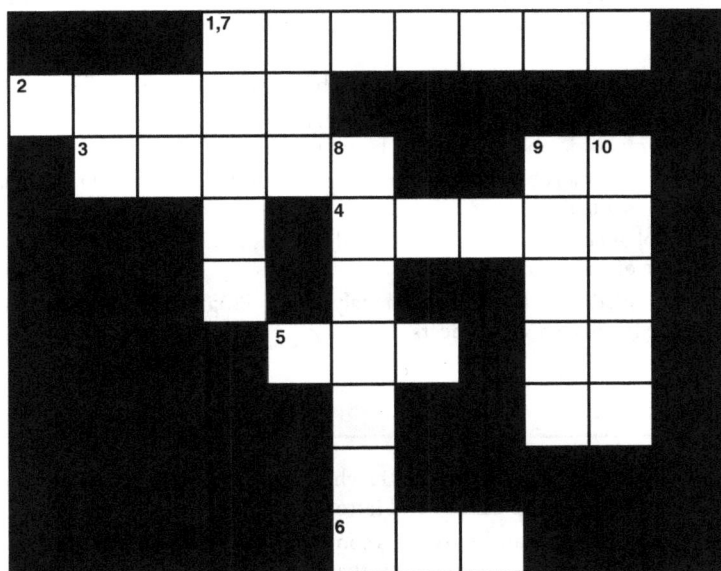

ACROSS

1. It was advertised using a television commercial featuring a tune composed by John Barry, "The girl with the sun in her hair" during the 1960s.
2. Current day successor to the Waterbury Clock Company, founded in 1854.
3. Humanoid robot created by Honda.
4. Started as a subsidiary of Tata Oil Mills on the request of Pt. Jawahar Lal Nehru.
5. Global Foundries was created by the divestiture of the manufacturing side of this company.
6. Founded in 1972 as Systemanalyse and Programmentwicklung by five former IBM engineers.

DOWN

7. The company started in 1881, when Kintar Hattori opened a watch and jewelry shop called "K. Hattori" in Tokyo.
8. The first corporate logo of this company was TOKIWA, derived from Tokiwa Shokai, the company that the founder, Takeshi Yamashita, had worked for.
9. It was the first watch on the moon, worn by Neil Armstrong and Buzz Aldrin.
10. Started in 1918 with a dozen Model T Ford cars in Chicago.

Crossword 2

ACROSS

1. Texas-based chain of American mid-range department stores where Sam Walton worked before starting Walmart.
2. The motto "Nation shall speak peace unto Nation" of this organization is generally attributed to Montague John Rendall, former headmaster of Winchester College and is said to be a "felicitous adaptation" of Micah 4: 3 "nation shall not lift up a sword against nation".
3. Japanese automobile company whose name means "fifty bells".
4. First major product of this company was the yubiwa pipe, a finger ring that would hold a cigarette, allowing the wearer to smoke the cigarette down to its nub while also leaving the wearer's hands free.

DOWN

5. Derives its name from the Taíno word for 'tobacco'.
6. Cole Haan, a fashion label that was founded in Chicago in 1928, is a wholly owned subsidiary of this company.
7. The name of this French company is a Catalan diminutive of the name of the first son, Daniel Carasso of the founder.
8. Best known for his role in creating Lotus Notes, he founded "FUSE Labs" (Future Social Experiences) within Microsoft to focus on innovation around future social web experience in 2009.
9. UK-based manufacturer and retailer of luxury mobile phones that was formerly a wholly owned subsidiary of Nokia.
10. Headquarters of Airbus.

Crossword 3

ACROSS

1. Picking stocks that have already sunk to the bottom but still have some bounce in them.
2. Established in T. Nagar in 1928 by Chinnasamy Chetti, a weaver who belonged to the Padmasaliyar community.
3. In automobile history, the phrase 'Fix it again, Tony' was popular mocking of this famous brand in its early years during its launch in the US.
4. "You'll wonder where the yellow went" is a slogan coined by Foote, Cone & Blender during the late 1940s for this brand.
5. According to Unilever records, it was the world's first registered brand and is therefore the world's oldest continuously existing brand.

DOWN

6. Carla Bruni is heiress to the fortune created by this Italian manufacturing company.
7. 'A Testament of a Furniture Dealer' is a manifesto written in 1976 by this company's founder.
8. "Last time there was this much excitement about a tablet, it had some commandments written on it" – The Wall Street Journal.

   In response to the launch of this product was this famous quote published by WSJ.
9. 'Chirp' is the official developer conference of this company started by Jack Dorsey.
10. Rani Mukherjee's character works for this organization in 'No One Killed Jessica'.

Crossword 4

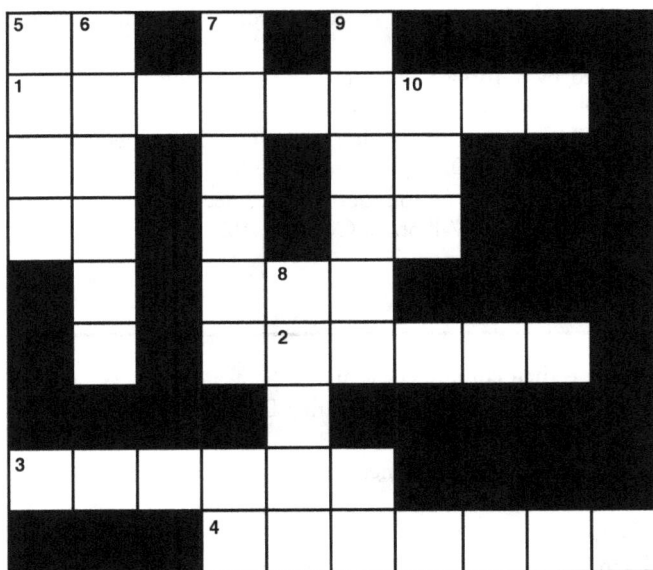

ACROSS

1. Card game that derives its name from a French word meaning 'Patience'.
2. Created by a Turkish software engineer having earned a Ph. D. in Computer Science from Stanford University.
3. First Chinese enterprise to join the Olympic Partner Programme of the International Olympic Committee (IOC).
4. Founded by Time co-founder Henry Luce in February 1930, four months after the Wall Street Crash of 1929.

DOWN

5. Antrix is their commercial arm.
6. Only motor scooter that the Harley-Davidson Motor Company ever produced.
7. 'The Triumph of the American Imagination' is a book about this synergistic empire.
8. Company that introduced safety belts.
9. Founded as the Swallow Sidecar Company by Sir William Lyons in 1922.
10. Business is their middle name.

Crossword 5

ACROSS

1. C in C.K. Prahalad.
2. Precision Optical Laboratory was this company's earlier name.
3. Launched in a converted factory in 1903 with $28,000 in cash from twelve investors, most notably John and Horace Dodge.
4. Barnes & Noble's answer to Kindle.
5. Creators of the diamond necklace for Yadavindra Singh, the Maharaja of Patiala.

DOWN

6. Listed on the Nasdaq Stock Market LLC® under the symbol ATX, the company was sold in 1916 to Walter R. Boss by the founder.
7. Ray Ozzie is this company's Chief Software Architect.
8. Founded by Mohammad Ali Jinnah in 1941 as a mouthpiece for the Muslim League.
9. Company that was founded in1882 by pharmacist Carl Paul Beiersdorf.
10. This company changed its name to Asahi Optical Company Ltd in 1938.

Answers

Crossword 1

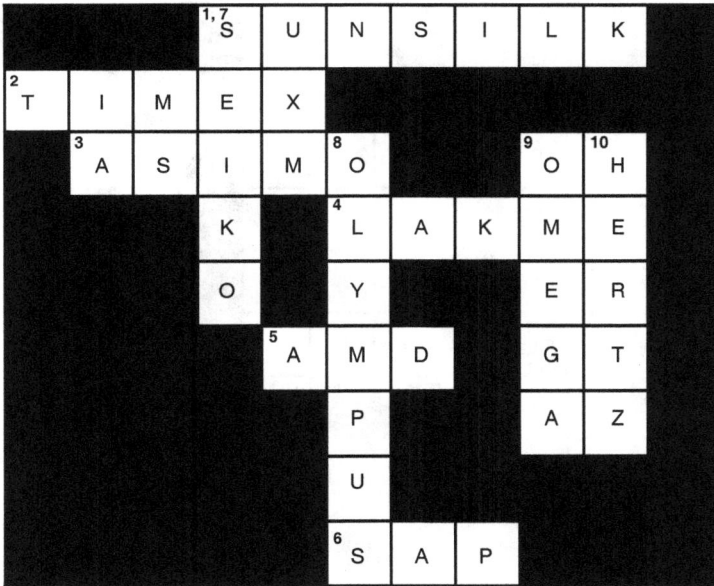

Answers

Crossword 2

				7 D	8 R			10 T
				A	A			O
1 J	5 C	P	E	6 N	N	Y		9 V	O
	O			I	O	Z		E	U
	H			K	N	Z		R	L
	I			E	E	Z		T	O
	2 B	B	C			3 I	S	U	Z	U
4 C	A	S	I	O		E			S
									E

Answers

Crossword 3

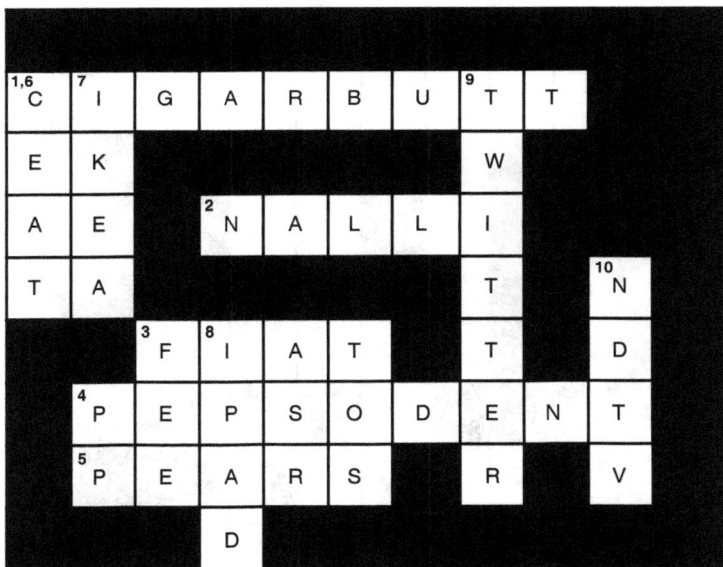

1,6 C	**7** I	G	A	R	B	U	**9** T	T
E	K						W	
A	E		**2** N	A	L	L	I	
T	A					T		**10** N
		3 F	**8** I	A	T	T		D
	4 P	E	P	S	O	D	E	N	T
	5 P	E	A	R	S		R		V
		D						

Answers

Crossword 4

⁵I	⁶T		⁷D		⁹J			
¹S	O	L	I	T	A	¹⁰I	R	E
R	P		S		G	B		
O	P		N		U	M		
	E		E	⁸V	A			
	R		Y	²O	R	K	U	T
				L				
³L	E	N	O	V	O			
			⁴F	O	R	T	U	N	E

Answers

Crossword 5

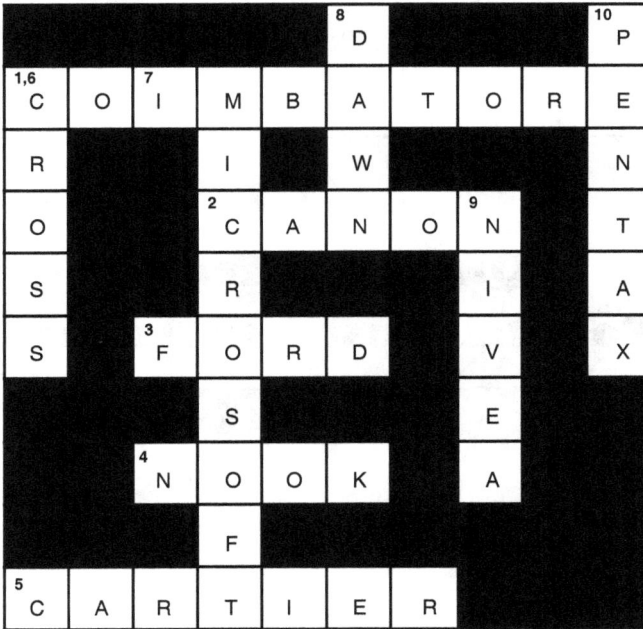

✠✠✠

Section VII

Questions from
Popular Business Quizzes

Brand Equity

1. For performing which Indian dance would you buy Kasavu sarees?
   a. Bihu
   b. Kathak
   c. Mohiniattam

2. If 16 annas = 1 Rupee then Rs. 15 =................
   a. 1 Mohur
   b. 1 Cowry
   c. 1 Cent

3. According to Peter Drucker, all companies have only 2 functions, viz. Marketing and ....
   a. Innovation
   b. Ideation
   c. Segmentation

4. Monopsony is a situation where there is only one
   a. Banker
   b. Buyer
   c. Seller

5. Which was the first international brand to support-Save Your Logo, a campaign launched in October 2008 with the help of the Global Environment Facility, the World Bank and the International Union for Conservation of Nature, which aims for major firms to help conserve the species used in their logo?
   a. WWF
   b. Puma
   c. Lacoste

6. In which country is Tolo TV present?
   a. Afghanistan
   b. Bhutan
   c. Pakistan

7. Which of these companies had to buy the rights for their name from a hotel chain?
    a. Wipro
    b. Google
    c. Intel

8. A consumer .... water, ... bottled water, ...bisleri.
    a) Wants, Needs, Demands
    b) Needs, Wants, Demands
    c) Demands, Needs, Wants

9. Which product is traditionally taken in 'Copita'?
    a) Espresso Coffee
    b) Sherry
    c) Tequila

10. In the early 1920s, the Standard Oil tanker J.A. Moffet became the first ship to use an ....?
    a) Radar
    b) Lady Hostess
    c) Autopilot

11. Which city's name appears below the brand name Haldiram?

12. What common thing that you find in most of the households is also known as a Devil's Ivy?

13. Worcestershire sauce was first made in England, but in which country did it originate?

14. What replaced the king's image on Nepalese Rs 500 note?

15. Complete this quote by Peter Drucker "The productivity of work is not the responsibility of the worker but of the ...."

16. Written on 168 palm leaves, which famous manuscript was discovered by Bhatta Swamy of Tanjore in 1900?

17. Which city serves as the location of headquarters of the most number of Fortune 500 companies?

18. Which industry has largest number of customers for robotics?

19. Where would you find the first writtten rule for apprenticeship?

20. Which bank's official estimate of the size of economies is known as the Atlas Method?

21. Which was the first company to have a celebrity spokesperson?

22. How much does it cost for an adult tourist to enter the White House?

23. Which brand of beer has the highest market share in Australia?
24. The world's largest corporate training centre located in India, belongs to which company?
25. World's largest solar powered kitchen cooks enough food to feed 15,000 people a day. In which Indian city is it located?
26. Which planet is named after the ancient roman god of trade and profit?
27. In America, 8 out of 10 .... products are sold at parties. Fill in the blank.
28. If 'Kingfisher Beer' is from India, then 'San Miguel Beer' is from which country?
29. Why did Steve Jobs sell all his Apple stocks except one after disagreement with John Sculley?
30. What kind of buzzword is "Fuzzword"?
31. In which historic landmark building in New York City is the old Waldorf-Astoria Hotel housed?
32. Microsoft has patented a technology called SPOT. If S is Smart and T is Technology, what does PO stand for?
33. Who is the first ever winner of the World Food Prize?
34. In recycling industry, what does MSW stand for?
35. What is the opposite of an OTC drug?
36. The popular brands of what are 'Cashyo', 'Reals', and 'Big Boss'?
37. According to Ogilvy, "Great hospitals do two things: They look after patients, and ...."
38. Rose Director collaborated with her husband and wrote the book 'Free to choose'. Who is her famous husband?
39. In business hierarchy, what is marzipan layer?
40. • Dharavi : Mumbai
    • Bronx : New York
    • Faveks : ?

Answers

1. Mohiniattam
2. Mohur
3. Innovation
4. Buyer
5. Lacoste
6. Afghanistan
7. Intel
8. Needs, Wants, Demands
9. Sherry
10. Autopilot
11. Nagpur
12. Money Plant
13. India
14. Mount Everest
15. Manager
16. Arthashastra
17. New York
18. Automobile
19. The Code of Hammurabi
20. World Bank
21. Coca Cola
22. Free of Cost
23. Victoria Bitter
24. Infosys
25. Tirupati
26. Mercury
27. Tupperware
28. Philippines
29. To receive annual reports
30. Buzzword that confuses everybody
31. Empire State Building
32. Personal Objects
33. M.S. Swaminathan

34. Municipal Solid Waste
35. Prescription Drug
36. Fenny
37. They teach young doctors
38. Milton Friedman
39. The level of executives just below the partners in a firm
40. Rio De Janeiro

✠✠✠

Tata Crucible

Difficulty Level I

1. Name the Dutch giant that sells senseo coffee maker and sensor electric shavers.
2. What is Virgin's low cost airline in Australia called?
3. Which auto giant calls it fuel efficient models as 'Blue motion'?
4. Antrix is the commercial/marketing wing of which Indian organization?
5. Who passed from London School of Economics in 1923 and wrote the book "The problem with the Indian Rupee?
6. Prince Al Waheed is the first individual to order this product from Airbus. Name the product.
7. Which company advertises as "The Signature Pen since 1913"?
8. RADS is a defence company belonging to which country?
9. Which steel plant was inaugurated by Jawaharlal Nehru on the banks of Damodhar river valley?
10. "Tel Bhavan" is the corporate HQ of which oil PSU major that is situated at Dehradun?
11. Which watch brand is advertised with slogan "it takes a licking and keeps ticking"?
12. Who was named TIME person of the year in 1982?
13. The founder originally thought of 11, then extended to 21 and finally to 31. What?
14. Who was the financial advisor to Arnold Schwarzenegger in his California Senate elections?
15. Which fictional reporter started his career in 'La Petit'?
16. KOSPI is the representative stock market index of which sovereign state?
17. Which company was started in 1888 by Robert Wood along with James Wood and Edward Mead with their first product being sterile surgical dressings?

18. Which company's FoMoCo parts division sells aftermarket parts under the Motorcraft brand name?

19. 'Bada' is a mobile OS which derives its name from Korean word for Ocean. Which company developed it?

20. Who handed over first Maruti 800 car to Harpal Singh?

Difficulty Level II

1. Which Finnish software engineer claims that he is half "Nobel-prize-winning chemist" and half "blanket-carrying cartoon character"?

2. Which retail company founded by Otto Bershem has the tagline "Spirit of Commerce"?

3. What was launched at 5:00 p.m. EST on Sunday 1 June 1980 after an introduction by Ted Turner? Its main slogan is "The Most Trusted Name in News".

4. Toughbook is a trademarked brand name owned by which company? Toughbook refers to its line of semi-rugged and rugged laptop computers.

5. Based in Ahmedabad, which pharmaceutical company was promoted by U.N. Mehta initially as Trinity Laboratories Ltd?

6. Which group has its origins in 1900, when Dewan Bahadur A M M Chettiar established a money-lending and banking business in Burma?

7. Which respected inventor, Electrical engineer, dubbed as the father of Physics, lived his last 10 years in 3327 of Hotel New Yorker?

8. Which organisation get its name from the term "Research and Development"? They invented a telecommunication techinque which formed the basis of modern computer network.

9. Which respected, learned institute has a stained glass window as its logo and the motto is "Nullius in Verba" meaning "On the words of no one"?

10. Who began delivering motivational lectures, and built a successful business around motivational speaking, which he has incorporated as Qualified Learning Systems?

11. This beverage was invented by Walgreens' employee Ivar "Pop" Coulson in 1922 and now is very popular after meals. Identify.

12. Which is the official footwear of the Woodstock music festival?

13. Leukos Films is a production company launched in September 2007 by which Indian actor? It's first release was Evano Oruvan, which was released commercially in December 2007 .

14. Which was the only private limited company during World War II to supply fighter aircrafts to the German Airforce Luftwaffe?

15. In which legendary campaign ("Where's the Beef?") did elderly actress Clara Peller feature at the age of 81?

16. Which magazine was started by Bob Guccione in 1965?

17. Which company traces its origin to a small company called Natone started in 1930 by Emanuel Stolaroff?

18. Which GM company originally manufactured sewing machines and bicycles?

19. Which company was started in East London in 1843 by Charles Henry with the intention of selling tea?

20. Oryx FM is their Radio arm. Name the TV arm.

Difficulty Level III

1. Coined in 1972 by Wang Chuk, it is based on the idea that the true development of a society only happens when material and spiritual development happens concurrently. Identify the term.

2. Which term used in trade union negotiations was coined by Beatrice Webb in the 19th century?

3. Neal Stephenson's novel 'Snow Crash' defines a world by the name of Meta Verse. How do we better know it?

4. A gentleman by the name of Henry was bored with writing letters. So he went and bought a Lithographic printer and created what in 1846?

5. This phrase originated in a newsletter published by Arlene and Jose Ramos. It was created for the emerging pre-press industry going electronic in the late 1970s. After 3 years of publishing, the newsletter was sold to employees at the Stanford Research Institute in California. What phrase are we talking about?

6. Believed to be the oldest surviving logo in this industry, it is based on a doodle made by W. W. Hodkinson during a meeting with Adolph Zukor and is said to be based on the memories of his childhood in Utah. Identify the company whose logo's origin has been described.

7. What do you mean by Agflation, a term coined by Merrill Lynch?

8. In a letter to George Bernard Shaw in 1935, he writes:
"... you have to know that I believe myself to be writing a book on economic theory which will largely revolutionize – not, I suppose, at once but in the course of the next ten years – the way the world thinks about economic problems." Identify him.

9. How do we popularly know the 9-digit Standard Numbering code created by Gordon Foster, now Emeritus Professor of Statistics at Trinity College, Dublin for W.H. Smith and others in 1966?

10. Carl Barks published this first in 1947. The main theme of the book which was sort of a "financial fable" was what happens in a society where everyone becomes a millionaire. What was the name of the protagonist?

11. What is V-mail that was used during the World War II in America?

12. What is concorde effect?

13. The brand got its name from the royal banner of medieval France which was traditionally unfurled only on the battlefield and accompanied by the war cry Montjoie Saint Denis. Identify the brand.

14. Only two executives of a company know where this secret is stored. Another two have access of it. Only a handful of people know who the earlier mentioned people are. They are never allowed to travel together. Which secret is so well kept for more than 68 years?

15. Baburao Painter's Maharashtra Film Company, based in Kolhapur, had made a name for itself with its silent films in early 1920s. In 1920, the head of operations resigned from the company and Pendharkar's cousin Shantaram Vanakudre joined the company and became Baburao Painter's right-hand man. They started which famous company whose name means "beginning" or "dawn" in Hindi?

16. Which brand was founded in 1973 by Gordon and Rena Merchant and takes its name from the same word meaning a stagnant body of water attached to a waterway?

17. Sir Isaac Pitman developed the most widely used system of shorthand, known now as Pitman shorthand. He first proposed this in Stenographic Soundhand in 1837. It was followed in 1840 by 'Phonography' that is often referred to as the Penny Plate. What is the claim to fame of this publication?

18. Which city's name literally translate to merchants' harbour?

19. What is meant by the term "Wrap rage"?

20. Whose book 'Poverty and Un-British Rule in India' brought attention to the draining of India's wealth into Britain?

Answers

Difficulty Level I

1. Philips
2. Virgin Blue
3. Volkswagen
4. ISRO
5. Dr. B.R. Ambedkar
6. Airbus A380
7. Sheaffer
8. Israel
9. Bokaro Steel Plants
10. ONGC
11. Timex
12. Computer
13. Baskin Robbins "31 Flavors"
14. Warren Buffet
15. Tintin
16. South Korea
17. Johnson and Johnson
18. Ford Motor Company
19. Samsung
20. Indira Gandhi

Difficulty Level II

1. Linus Torvalds
2. Metro
3. Cable News Network (CNN)
4. Panasonic
5. Torrent Pharmaceuticals Ltd
6. Murugappa Group
7. Tesla
8. RAND Corporation
9. Royal Society of London
10. Shiva Khera
11. Milkshakes
12. Burkinstock Sandals

13. Madhavan
14. Messerschmitt
15. Wendy's
16. Penthouse
17. Neutrogena
18. Opel
19. Harrods
20. Al Jazeera

Difficulty Level III

1. Gross National Happiness
2. Collective Bargaining
3. Second Life
4. Hallmark Greeting Cards
5. WYSIWYG (What You See Is What You Get)
6. Paramount Pictures
7. An increase in the price of food that occurs as a result of increased demand from human consumption and use as an alternative energy resource.
8. John Maynard Keynes
9. ISBN
10. Scrooge
11. To reduce the logistics of transferring an original letter across the military postal system, a V-mail letter would be censored, copied to film, and printed back to paper upon arrival at its destination.
12. It refers to the human tendency to futilely persevere with an enterprise once we've invested money, time, or effort.
13. Oriflame
14. Formula for Coca-Cola
15. Prabhat Studios
16. Billabong
17. First ever correspondence course
18. Copenhagen
19. Wrap rage, also called package rage, is the common name for heightened levels of anger and frustration resulting from the inability to open hard-to-remove packaging, particularly some heat sealed plastic blister packs and clamshells.
20. Dadabhai Naoroji

✠ ✠ ✠

Section VIII
Facts

Firsties First

1. First ice cream brand to be taken into space aboard the Space Shuttle – Ben & Jerry's
2. First animated movie – The Toy Story
3. First glue stick – Pritt (by Henkel)
4. First ISO 9002 certified retail outlet of India – Landmark, Chennai (book-cum music store)
5. First billionaire – John D. Rockfeller
6. First James Bond novel to be adapted as a daily comic strip – Casino Royale
7. First advertising agency of India – Dattaram Advertising Pvt. Ltd.
8. First commercially available laundry detergent – Persil
9. First scratch-proof watch – Rado Diastar
10. First British fixed trust – Unit Trust
11. First museum in the world to be dedicated to a fictional character – The Sherlock Holmes Museum in Baker Street, London
12. First company on Wall Street to publish an annual fiscal report in 1941 – Merrill Lynch
13. First FMCG brand in India to channel its brand communication through podcasting – Frito Lays
14. First Sunday newspaper – The Observer
15. First 24-hour news channel – CNN
16. First ATMs in India were introduced by – HSBC
17. First Indian daily to introduce colour – The Hindu
18. First company to have CMM Level 5 certification in the world – Indian unit of Motorola (1993)
19. First GPRS cell phone developer – Motorola
20. First liquid nail polish brand – Cutex
21. First woman governor of Pakistan's Central Bank – Shamshad Akhtar
22. First company to manufacture computers for commercial use – Remington Rand

23. First computer was installed in India at – Indian Statistical institute, Kolkata
24. First woman to become the director of Bombay Stock Exchange – Deena Mehta
25. First Indian PSU disinvestment – Modern Foods
26. First Public Sector company to become Private company – Maruti Udyog
27. First Indian actress to model for Lux – Leela Chitnis
28. First Hollywood actress to model for Lux – Ginger Rogers
29. First Indian cricketer to model for a brand – Farookh Engineer
30. First scooter manufacturer – Piaggio

✠ ✠ ✠

Logos & Famous Brands

EVOLUTION

Apple Inc.

(1976)   (1976 - 1998)   (1998)   Current Logo

The first Apple logo was designed by Ron Wayne, co-founder of Apple Computer. It showed Sir Isaac Newton sitting beneath the famous Apple tree thinking about gravity.

It was only used for the Apple I. Steve Jobs felt that it was too intellectual and it was almost impossible to put on computers as one could only recognize the details of the drawing when it was large enough.

Almost immediately, though, this was replaced by Rob Janoff's "rainbow Apple", the now-familiar rainbow-coloured silhouette of an apple with a bite taken out of it. Janoff presented Jobs with several different monochromatic themes for the "bitten" logo, and Jobs immediately took a liking to it. While Jobs liked the logo, he insisted it be in colour to humanize the company. The Apple logo was designed with a bite so that it wouldn't be recognized as another fruit. The coloured stripes were conceived to make the logo more accessible, and to represent the fact the monitor could reproduce images in colour.

In 1998, with the roll-out of the new iMac, Apple discontinued the rainbow theme and began to use monochromatic themes, nearly identical in shape to its previous rainbow incarnation, on various products, packaging and advertising. An Aqua-themed version of the monochrome logo was used from 2001–2003, and a Glass-themed version has been used since 2003.

Canon Inc.

In 1933, when Precision Optical Instruments Laboratory was established, the name given to the cameras manufactured on a trial basis at the time was Kwanon. This title reflected the benevolence of Kwanon, the Buddhist Goddess of Mercy, and embodied the company's vision of creating the best cameras in the world. The logo included the word with an image of "Kwanon with 1,000 Arms" and flames.

When the company sought to begin full-scale marketing, it needed a brand name that would be accepted by people worldwide. From this standpoint, in 1935 the name Canon was registered as the official trademark. The word Canon has a number of meanings, including scriptures, criterion and standard. The trademark was therefore worthy of a company involved with precision equipment, where accuracy is fundamentally important. It also embodied the company's desire to meet world-class criteria and industry standards. And since Canon and Kwanon had similar pronunciations, the transition went smoothly.

Timeline
1934. The engraved Kwanon logo was used on the cameras trial-manufactured by the Company (but not actually released in the market).

1935. The Canon logo is registered as a trademark. Prominent features were already inherent in the refinement process.

1953. Unification of the logo. The image was further refined to achieve an overall balance.

1956. The current logo was the culmination of painstaking and meticulous design efforts.

Eastman Kodak Company

Kodak's origins rest with Eastman Dry Plate Company, and the General Aristo Company, founded by inventor George Eastman in Rochester and Jamestown, New York. The General Aristo Company was formed in 1899 in Jamestown New York, with George Eastman as treasurer, and this company purchased the stock of American Aristotype Company. George Eastman registered the trademark Kodak on September 4, 1888. The Eastman Kodak Company was founded by Eastman in 1892. He also coined the advertising slogan, "You press the button, we do the rest."

Timeline

1900's. Kodak is the first company to integrate its name and look into a symbol.

1930's. Focus moved to the Kodak name and the red and yellow "trade dress" colour.

1960's. The corner curl was introduced.

1970's. The mark retained the red and yellow colours and the Kodak name, but a box and graphic "K" element were added.

1980's. A more contemporary type font streamlined the Kodak name within the existing logo.

Today. The box is gone, simplifying the logo. The rounded type font and distinctive "a" give the name a more contemporary look.

Google Inc.

The clarity of thought is visible in the company's logo right from the very beginning, when in 1996 two Stanford University computer science graduate students Larry Page and Sergey Brin built the search engine.

The name of the search engine is derived from Googol (meaning one followed by 100 zeros). Google's first logo was created by Sergey Brin, after he taught himself to use the free graphic software GIMP. Later, an exclamation mark mimicking the Yahoo! logo was added.

In 1999, Stanford's Consultant Art Professor Ruth Kedar designed the Google logo that the company uses today.

IBM

In 1911, the International Time Recording Company (ITR, est. 1888) and the Computing Scale Company (CSC, est. 1891) merged to form the Computing-Tabulating-Recording Company.

In 1924, the company adopted the name International Business Machines Corporation and a new modern-looking logo. It made employee time-keeping systems, weighing scales, meat slicers, and punched-card tabulators.

In the late 1940s, IBM began a difficult transition of punched-card tabulating to computers, led by its CEO Thomas J. Watson. To signify this radical change, in 1947, IBM changed its logo for the first time in over two decades: a simple typeface logo.

In 1956, with the leadership of the company being passed down to Watson's son, Paul Rand changed IBM's logo to have "a more solid, grounded and balanced appearance" and at the same time he made the change subtle enough to communicate that there's continuity in the passing of the baton of leadership from father to son.

IBM logo's last big change – which wasn't all that big – was in 1972, when Paul Rand replaced the solid letters with horizontal stripes to suggest "speed and dynamism."

Mazda Motor Corporation

Mazda began as the Toyo Cork Kogyo Co., Ltd, founded in Japan in 1910. Toyo Cork Kogyo renamed itself to Toyo Kogyo Co., Ltd. in 1927.

Toyo Kogyo moved from manufacturing machine tools to vehicles, with the introduction of the Mazda-Go in 1931. Toyo Kogyo produced weapons for the Japanese military throughout the Second World War, most notably the series 30 through 35 Type 99 rifle. The company formally adopted the Mazda name in 1984, though every automobile sold from the beginning bore that name. The Mazda R360 was introduced in 1960, followed by the Mazda engines in 1962.

Similar to the emblem of Hiroshima city, the Mazda logo introduced in 1936 expresses Mazda's strong links to its hometown of Hiroshima. The three mountains (representing Hiroshima) form the Latin alphabet letter M, which is duplicated three times for "Mazda Motor Manufacturer". The long side extensions represent wings for agility and speed.

In 1991, Mazda adopted a corporate symbol which was to represent a sun and a flame standing for heartfelt passion. This is commonly referred to in Mazda enthusiast circles as the "cylon" logo.

Shortly after the release of the new symbol, the design was smoothed out to reduce its similarity to Renault's and the "eternal flame" logo was introduced.

The current logo is a stylised "M" meant to show Mazda stretching its wings for the future.

Microsoft Corporation

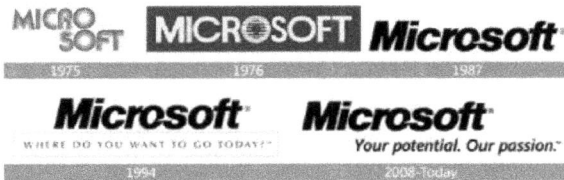

Microsoft is also one of those companies that always went with typography for their brand icon. After the initial groovy logo, they changed it to the so called "Blibbet" Logo in 1975 but it got replaced by the "Pac-Man" Logo, designed by Scott Baker and used since 1987. Since then Microsoft tried to add two different slogans and is now using "Your potential. Our passion." with the "Pac-Man" Logo.

Renault S.A.

Louis Renault was 21 when he made his first car in the backyard of his parent's home. He soon got orders for cars, so in 1898, along with his brothers and friends, Louis opened the company Société Renault Frères in Boulogne-Billancourt, France.

The first Renault logo, drawn in 1900 featured the three initials of the Renault brothers: Louis, Ferdinand and Marcel.

In 1906, the logo changed to a front end of a car enclosed in a gear wheel.

During World War I, Renault manufactured light tanks for the Allies called the Renault FT-17. This was so popular that after the war, Renault actually changed its logo into a tank.

The diamond shape logo was introduced in 1925 and remained until today. The modern Renault logo was created in 1972 by Victor Vasarely, the father of Op-art.

Škoda_Auto

Skoda, is an automobile manufacturer based in Czech Republic. It became a subsidiary of the Volkswagen Group in 1991. The company was started as a bicycle manufacturing company back in 1890s. Vaclav Laurin and Václav Klement started a bicycle repair shop in Mladá Boleslav (1895), and later they started a bicycle and motorcycle manufacturing factory in 1898. The company's first logo was based on the Slavia brand, with lime leaves, to represent the Slav nations. The logo also included the owners' names which later became the main foundation for future logos.

In 1905, "L&K" logo (initials of the owners) was designed and was influenced by Art Nouveau, an artistic style at the beginning of the 20th century. From 1926, the cars were produced under the brand name Skoda, which is reflected in the oval shaped logo of the company. The laurels enclosing the brand name were retained in the new logo as well.

The famous "winged arrow" logo was first introduced in 1926, but its origin and designer is unknown. This was merged with the Skoda brand logo and the new logo was used on cars from 1990.

Xerox Corporation

The Xerox Company used to be known as the Haloid Company almost 100 years ago. But in 1938, Chester Carlson invented a technique called xerography which we today call the photocopy technique. Unfortunately no one was willing to invest in his invention, and many big giants like IBM, GE, RCA and others decided not to finance this invention.

But Haloid Company decided to go with Chester and made the first photocopying machine named Haloid Xerox 14. As can be seen in their logos, the original Haloid word which was prominent in the company's logo before 1961 was completely replaced by Xerox due to the immense success of this idea.

They retained almost the same logo from 1961 to 2004. But in 2004 there was a problem with the Xerox books and it tried to reinvent itself with a new logo. People associate the company only with photocopy machines, and that has been a major problem for Xerox.

The company changed its logo in 2008 to get away from this stereotyped image, by changing the font of the word. They also added a ball which has a stylish X instead of their 'boring' X in earlier times.

OLD LOGOS

➤ Pontiac is named after Chief Pontiac, an Ottawa leader who became famous for his role in Pontiac's Rebellion (1763–1766), an American Indian struggle against the British military occupation of the Great Lakes region following the British victory in the French and Indian War.

A Native American headdress was used as a logo until 1956. The American Indian headdress is obviously connected to Chief Pontiac referenced earlier. The American Indian headdress was updated to the currently used Native American red arrowhead design for 1957. The arrowhead logo is also known as the Dart.

➤ The earliest Nestlé logo was introduced by Henri Nestlé in 1868, based on the meaning of his name in German, i.e. little nest, as an artistic conceptualisation of his family emblem. Henri secured a 15-year French patent for this design the same year. Following his retirement, the logo was registered in Vevey in 1875 by the new owners of the Nestlé S.A. company.

➤ The Buick trishield is rooted in the ancestral coat of arms of the automaker's founder, David Dunbar Buick. That crest was a red shield with a checkered silver and azure diagonal line from the upper left to lower right, a stag above and a punctured cross below. The division adopted this on its radiator grilles in 1937.

➤ Though BBC was created in 1922, a formal BBC brand did not evolve until fairly late in the corporation's history. Initially, a mix of straight type or decorative design motifs were used – see for example the elaborate tracery of the initials found on the mosaic floor of the original reception of Broadcasting House (opened 1932).

The first attempt at a proper brand image came in 1953, when Abram Games was commissioned to design an on-air image, probably hastened by the imminent arrival of commercial competition. Games, who designed the logo for the Festival of Britain in 1951, created the logo nicknamed the 'Bat's wings' logo, an elegant and rather ethereal image which captured the spirit of the times.

➤ P&G's former logo originated in 1851 as a crude cross that barge workers on the Ohio River painted on cases of P&G star candles to identify them. P&G later altered this symbol into a trademark that showed a man in the moon overlooking 13 stars, said to commemorate the original 13 colonies.

The company received unwanted media publicity in the 1980s when rumours spread that the moon-and-stars logo was a satanic symbol. These interpretations have been denied by the company officials, and no evidence linking the company to the Church of Satan or any other occult organization has ever been presented.

➤ In 1898, one year after the establishment of Nippon Gakki Co. Ltd., forerunner to today's Yamaha Corporation, the company decided to use a tuning fork as its corporate mark, with "a design featuring a hoo (Chinese phoenix) holding a tuning fork in its mouth" as the trademark. Since then, after undergoing a variety of changes that paralleled the growth of the company, the tuning fork mark was finally unified in 1967.

➤ The first Opel logo was designed after the founding of the company consisted of the squiggly letters A and O, the initials of Adam Opel. The A was in bronze, the O kept in red.

➤ Supposedly, the famous Fiat "scrabble tiles" logo of the 1960s was designed by the company's Chief Designer who was driving past the Fiat factory during a power outage and saw an outline of the factory's neon sign against the dark sky.

FUN FACTS

➤ The slanted E in Dell's logo represents Michael Dell's wish to turn the world on its ear.

➤ The FedEx wordmark is notable for containing a hidden right-pointing arrow in the negative space between the "E" and the "X", which was achieved by designing a proprietary font, based on Univers and Futura, to emphasize the arrow shape.

➤ Since 2000, Amazon's logotype is an arrow leading from A to Z, representing customer satisfaction (as it forms a smile); a goal was to have every product in the alphabet.

➤ The image of a bear is hidden in the Matterhorn mountain of Toblerone chocolates symbolizing the town of its origin – Bern. According to the local legend, based on folk etymology, the founder of the city of Bern, vowed to name the city after the first animal he met on the hunt, and this turned out to be a bear.

➤ The livery of Singapore Airlines includes the "bird" (also known as the Silver Kris) logo on the tailfin, which has remained unchanged since Singapore Airlines' inception, but the logotype and stripes used since 1972 were changed in 1988 to the ones still in use today.

➤ Carrefour means crossroads in French. The logo features the letter "C" between two arrows that point in different directions.

➤ Sun Microsystems logo, which features four interleaved copies of the word sun, was designed by professor Vaughan Pratt of Stanford University.

➤ The Baskin-Robbins ice cream parlours started as separate ventures from Burt Baskin and Irv Robbins, owning Burt's Ice Cream Shop and Snowbird Ice Cream respectively. Snowbird Ice Cream featured 21 flavours, a novel concept for the time. When the separate companies merged in 1953, this concept grew to 31 flavours.

➤ The VAIO logo represents the integration of analog and digital technology with the 'VA' representing an analog wave and the 'IO' representing a digital binary code.

➤ The three diamonds of the Mitsubishi logo is actually the graphical representation of the literal translation of the company name, "mitsu" meaning three and "hishi", from 'bishi', meaning diamonds. These three diamonds signify integrity, reliability, and trust that the company tries to build with its customers by providing them a safe and eco-compatible car range.

➤ The Hyundai logo appears in an oval shaped H with an ellipse outline, which indicates the company's global expansion. The stylised, slanted "H" on the other hand, symbolises two people, the customer and the company, shaking hands.

➤ A three-pointed star in a circle clearly reminds of Mercedes Benz. The logo indicates the ability of its motors to conquer all the three realms viz. land, air and sea.

➤ The logo of Toyota consists of three ellipses that represent the heart of the product, the heart of the customer and the constant technological growth and boundless opportunities that are to be tapped.

➤ The famous Coca-Cola logo was created by John Pemberton's bookkeeper, Frank Mason Robinson, in 1885. Robinson came up with the name and chose the logo's distinctive cursive script. The typeface used, known as Spencerian script, was developed in the mid 19th Century and was the dominant form of formal handwriting in the United States during that period.

➤ The Nike Swoosh logo was created in 1971 by graphic design student Carolyn Davidson, for $35.00, based on a billing rate of $2.00 per hour. Davidson did however, get more of a payday from the athletic company in 1983 when Nike gave Davidson a gold Swoosh gold ring and an envelope filled with an undisclosed amount of Nike stock to express their gratitude.

➤ The Volkswagen logo was the result of a 50 Marks office competition, won by an engineer named Franz Reimspiess (the same man who perfected the engine for the Beetle in the 1930's).

➤ In 1977, William S. Doyle, Deputy Commissioner of the New York State Department of Commerce recruited Milton Glaser, a productive graphic designer to work on the famous New York advertising campaign. Glaser expected the campaign to last only a couple months and did the work pro bono.

➤ The Rolling Stone lips logo has come to represent the legendary mouth of Mick Jagger but designer John Pascheis on record that the original inspiration came from an image of the Hindu goddess Kali. Pasche was paid £50 for his work at the time, but received the generous supplement of an extra £200 a couple of years later. The group themselves now own the copyright, but in 2006, Pasche sold the original artwork for £400,000.

➤ The concept for the recycling logo, designed by Gary Andersonin 1971, came from 19th century mathematician August Ferdinand Mobius, a name most of us will recognize when we talk about a Mobius strip, a strip of paper that when twisted into itself and joined at both ends forms an infinite loop. The recycling logo was designed as part of a contest for a Chicago-based cardboard packaging company and is used to represent recycled and recyclable packaging and goods.

➤ The Mr. Yuk logo was conceived by a Pittsburgh Doctor, Richard Moriarty, who created him as a poison warning for children. Before the design of Mr. Yuk, the standard poison warning label was a skull and crossbones, and Moriarity was concerned that children might confuse the symbol with the Jolly Rogers logo of The Pittsburgh

Pirates baseball team. The green colour theme was chosen when Moriarty was testing the logo with students, and one described a green version as "Yucky!" That's also where the name came from. Nationally, the Mr. Yuk symbol was adopted as a replacement for the traditional skull and crossbones warning label, because it was thought that many youngsters might identify the original mark with pirates and thus ignore the warning intended.

➤ Known as the "Drop-T" design, the now famous Beatles' logo was based on an impromptu sketch by instrument retailer and designer Ivor Arbiter in 1963. The logo was first used on the front of drummer Ringo Starr's bass drum, which Beatle's manager Brian Epstein and Starr purchased from Arbiter's London shop Drum City.

➤ The Google logo font is Catull BQ, and it was created for Berthold in 1982 by German designer Gustav Jaeger.

➤ The Lufthansa logo, an encircled stylized crane in flight, was created in 1918 by Otto Firle. It was part of the livery of the first German airline, Deutsche Luft-Reederei (abbreviated DLR), which began air service on 5 February 1919. In 1926 Deutsche Luft Hansa adopted this symbol, and in 1954 Lufthansa expressed continuity by adopted it, too.

➤ Chevrolet first used its "Bowtie emblem" logo in 1913. It is said to have been designed from wallpaper Durant once saw in a French hotel.

➤ BMW logo is a stylised representation of an airplane propeller spinning against the clear blue sky. It reflects the origins of BMW as a maker of military aircraft engines during World War I. Also, white and blue are the traditional colours of Bavaria.

➤ In 1862, Cuban wine merchant Facundo Bacardi, originating from Spain, acquired a distillery in Santiago de Cuba. This distillery used the method developed by Bacardi for refining sugar and liquor into a white coloured mild rum. Because there were a large number of bats living under the roof of the distillery, it was decided that it was appropriate to also show the bats on the brand of its white Bacardi Rum products.

✠ ✠ ✠

Tata World

1. 'Spice' is a quarterly culinary guide from Taj Hotels Resorts and Palaces that includes updates on the latest culinary offerings at the Taj restaurants and also traces the continual endeavours of Taj to bring guests a new medley of gourmet experiences.

2. The Tata Institute of Social Sciences (TISS) was established in 1936, as the Sir Dorabji Tata Graduate School of Social Work.

3. Tata Sumo is said to have got its name from Sumant Moolgaonkar, (Su-Mo) who was instrumental in a number of revolutionary changes in TELCO and bringing about significant progress.

4. Pune Industrial Hotels Limited was set up in 1964 by the Kirloskar Group for their first foray into hospitality. This company set up Hotel Blue Diamond in Pune and began to manage Hotel Pearl in Kolhapur. Hotel Blue Diamond was acquired by Indian Hotels in 1999.

5. Roots Corporation Limited (RCL) is a subsidiary of The Indian Hotels Company Limited (IHCL) that was incorporated to operate the first-of-its-kind category of Smart Basics™ hotel chain across the country called Ginger. The concept of Smart Basics™ hotel chain was developed in association with renowned corporate strategy thinker, Dr C. K. Prahalad.

6. J.R.D. Tata received the prestigious United Nations Population Award for 1992 from the Secretary General of the United Nations at the UN Headquaters in New York in September 1992.

7. R Gopalakrishnan is an Executive Director with Tata Sons. He is the author of two books – The Case of the Bonsai Manager and When the Penny Drops: Learning What's Not Taught.

8. Malabar Princess was the name of the first international flight by Air India from Bombay to London that took off in June 1948.

9. Kapil Ram Vakil had set up the Okha Salt works which failed at that time. He then appealed to the Tatas with the support of the Maharaja of Baroda that eventually led to the creation of Tata Chemicals.

10. Tata Indica, the first car made by the Tatas, is sold in UK under the name 'City Rover'.

11. TajSATS Air Catering Ltd. is a joint venture of the Indian Hotels Company, popularly known as the Taj Hotels Resorts and Palaces, and SATS (Singapore Airport Terminal Services).

12. Morris Travers, AG Bourne & MO Foster were the first three directors of the Indian Institute of Science, Bangalore, which was founded by the TATAs.

13. During the Second World War, armoured cars were fitted with bullet proof plates and rivets made by Tata Steel, called Tatanagars.

14. JRD was the trustee of Sir Dorabji Tata Trust from its inception in 1932 for over half a century. Under his guidance, this Trust established Asia's first cancer hospital, the Tata Memorial Center for Cancer, Research and Treatment, in Bombay in 1941. It also founded the Tata Institute of Social Sciences (TISS, 1936), the Tata Institute of Fundamental Research (TIFR, 1945), and the National Center for Performing Arts.

15. The Taj Mahal Palace hotel resort first opened its doors to guests on December 16, 1903. It is widely believed that Tata decided to build the luxurious hotel after he was refused entry to one of the city's grand hotels of the time, Watson's Hotel, as it was restricted to 'whites only'. The original Indian architects were Sitaram Khanderao Vaidya and D. N. Mirza, but the project was completed by an English engineer W. A. Chambers.

16. Burmah Shell was the company that had refuelled JRD Tata's plane in 1932, when he flew to Puss Moth from Karachi with a load of mail for Bombay.

17. New India Assurance was an insurance company that was established by the Tatas in 1919 with a capital of 20 crores.

18. Sir Ghulam Md. was a Tata Industries Director who was released of his responsibilities by the Tatas to become the first Finance Minister of Pakistan.

19.   TIFRAC (Tata Institute of Fundamental Research Automatic Calculator) was the first computer developed in India, at the Tata Institute of Fundamental Research in Mumbai. Initially, a TIFR Pilot Machine was developed in the 1950s. It was started in 1955 and commissioned in November 1956.

20.   On 1 February 1978, when JRD ceased to be the chairman of Air India, he wrote a famous letter to the staff published in their journal, which was called MAGIC CARPET.

21.   The claim to fame of Miss Genell Moots of TWA in the history of the Tatas is that JRD called her to train the first batch of air hostesses for Air India.

22.   Girish Wagh is Vice President & Head Small Car Project of Tata Motors. He is a key figure in the Tata Nano's project.

23.   TERI is today known as The Energy & Resources Institute. It was actually started by the Tatas in 1974, when it was known as Tata Energy Research Institute.

24.   Tata Airlines was founded in 1932 by J.R.D. Tata along with an Englishman Nevill Vintcent to fulfill an adolescent dream.

25.   The Tata Steel Adventure Foundation (TSAF) conducts sport such as rock-climbing, river-rafting and para-sailing. It is headed by a famous Indian-Bachendri Pal.

✠ ✠ ✠

Terminology

BUZZWORDS

➤ **Blamestorming:** A discussion (which may be at the group, community, or society level) in which members attempt to assign blame for a particular misdeed.

➤ **Blogsnob:** One who refuses to respond to comments on their blog from people outside their friends circle.

➤ **Bluejacking:** It refers to sending unnecessary and anonymous messages by using bluetooth enabled devices as a contact. It has been derived from bluetooth and hijacking.

➤ **Boss-Spasming:** Suddenly looking busy as a manager enters the room.

➤ **Cabinet castaways:** They are products bought by consumers and never used by them.

➤ **Cube Farm:** An office with umpteen number of cubicles.

➤ **Egosurfing:** Practice of searching for one's own given name, surname, full name, pseudonym, or screen name on a popular search engine, to see what results appear.

➤ **Fridge Googling:** Running an Internet search based on some or all of the contents of one's fridge, looking for a recipe based on those contents.

➤ **Fuel Collar Worker:** Those either in the travel industry or who very regularly travel as apart of their job, i.e. door to door salesmen, field salesmen, airline pilots, etc. They spend the bulk of their time traveling.

➤ **Grass Ceiling:** The disadvantage ladies might face in scaling the corporate ladder because of golf.

➤ **McDonaldization:** The process in which a society takes the characteristics of a fast food restaurant. The term was coined by George Ritzer.

➤ **Morganisation:** Organisational abilities to rescue failing firms and restore them to profits.

➤ **Pharming:** Rerouting the traffic of a particular website to a bogus one.

➤ **Qwerty Tummy:** It is a bad tummy brought on by the use of a filthy computer keyboard. A recent study showed that a keyboard has five times more bacteria than a toilet seat. The keyboard user could inadvertently put a finger in the mouth and suffer acute food poisoning. It all starts when people eat while working, leaving crumbs on the keyboard, which attract mice.

➤ **Silicon Valley Haircut:** The venture capitalist replacing the founder with a professional in an IT venture.

➤ **Sillywood:** Movies made by collaboration between Silicon Valley and Hollywood.

➤ **Sweethearting:** Sweethearting is a method cashiers use to pass on goods to friends by failing to bill one. They do so by passing two items, and obscuring the barcode of one, so it goes unnoticed.

➤ **Viagrisation:** In the world of advertising, it refers to the use of long sustained advertising campaign to promote an event which is essentially short in life. For example - IPL

➤ **Wardriving:** It is the act of searching for Wi-Fi wireless networks by a person in a moving vehicle, using a portable computer or PDA. Wardriving was named after the term wardialing from the 1983 film WarGames, which involved searching for computer systems with software that dialed numbers sequentially to see which ones were connected to a fax machine or computer.

➤ **Xerox Subsidy:** Euphemism for swiping free photocopies from one's workplace.

✠ ✠ ✠

MANAGEMENT TERMS & PRINCIPLES

1.	The most ineffective workers are systematically moved to the place where they can do the least damage.	Dilbert Principle
2.	A small percentage of a total is responsible for a large proportion of value of resources.	Pareto's Principle
3.	In a hierarchy, every employee tends to rise to his level of incompetence.	Peter Principle
4.	Work Expands to fill the time available for its completion	Parkinson's Law
5.	A technological innovation that improves a product or service in ways that the market does not expect, typically by being lower priced or designed for a different set of consumers.	Disruptive Technology
6.	A middle-class suburban woman who spends a significant amount of her time transporting her school-age children to activities such as soccer practice and music lessons.	Soccer Mom
7.	The small forces behind tomorrow's big changes	Micro Trends
8.	It is the effect by which one accidentally discovers something fortunate, especially while looking for something else entirely.	Serendipity
9.	An individual who with his skill and ability obtains temporary assignments in a variety of organizations rather than a permanent job.	Portfolio Worker
10.	A person who rolls part of the credit card bill over to the next month.	Revolver
11.	It is a bonus offered by hiring firms if the hired joins the company from a rival firm. It is very similar to the traditional joining bonus offered by firms but will be offered usually for rival firm employees luring them into a firm.	Golden Hello

12.	It is the practice of executing trades for an investment account by a salesman or broker in order to generate commission from the account.	Churning
13.	Any of a set of words that share the same numeric combination as another when typed using on a mobile phone that uses predictive text, e.g "home" and "good" both written on a cell phone key pad as 4663.	Textonym
14.	An informal name for an employment recruiter, sometimes referred to as Executive search.	Headhunter
15.	In a business setting, it comes at the beginning of a project rather than the end, so that the project can be improved rather than autopsied.	Premortem
16.	Abnormal market behaviour where consumers purchase the higher-priced goods whereas similar low-priced (but not identical) substitutes are available. It is caused either by the belief that higher price means higher quality, or by the desire for conspicuous consumption (to be seen as buying an expensive, prestige item).	Veblen Effect
17.	It is a type of organisation design with is temporary, adaptive, creative, in contrast with bureaucracy which tends to be relatively permanent, rule-driven and inflexible.	Adhocracy
18.	A personalized desktop portal that focuses on business intelligence and knowledge management.	Digital Dashboard
19.	It is an organizational structure where a core of essential executives and workers are supported by outside contractors and part-time help.	Shamrock Organisation

20.	It represents the mutual beliefs, perceptions, and informal obligations between an employer and an employee. It sets the dynamics for the relationship and defines the detailed practicality of the work to be done. It is distinguishable from the formal written contract of employment which, for the most part, only identifies mutual duties and responsibilities in a generalized form.	Psychological Contract
21.	This theory states that workers inherently dislike and avoid work and must be driven to it.	Theory X
22.	This theory states that work is natural and can be a source of satisfaction when aimed at higher order human psychological needs.	Theory Y
23.	This theory focused on increasing employee loyalty to the company by providing a job for life with a strong focus on the well-being of the employee, both on and off the job.	Theory Z
24.	A phenomenon discovered by Dr Meredith Belbin where teams of highly capable individuals can, collectively, perform badly.	Apollo Syndrome
25.	This is a fictional condition used to describe someone who believes that he or she can see the future but cannot do anything about it.	Cassandra Syndrome
26.	This theory is the "proposition that human behaviour is the function of both the person and the environment: expressed in symbolic terms, B = f (P, E)."	Field Theory
27.	In economics, this term refers to situations where the advancement of a qualified person within the hierarchy of an organization is stopped at a lower level because of some form of discrimination, most commonly sexism or racism.	Glass Ceiling
28.	Rise in currency value affecting business	Dutch Disease

Top 100 Advertising Campaigns of the Century

1.	Volkswagen	"Think Small"	Doyle Dane Bernbach	1959
2.	Coca-Cola	"The pause that refreshes"	D'Arcy Co.	1929
3.	Marlboro	The Marlboro Man	Leo Burnett Co.	1955
4.	Nike	"Just do it"	Wieden & Kennedy	1988
5.	McDonald's	"You deserve a break today"	Needham, Harper & Steers	1971
6.	DeBeers	"A diamond is forever"	N.W. Ayer & Son	1948
7.	Absolut Vodka	The Absolut Bottle	TBWA	1981
8.	Miller Lite beer	"Tastes great, less filling"	McCann-Erickson Worldwide	1974
9.	Clairol	"Does she...or doesn't she?"	Foote, Cone & Belding	1957
10.	Avis	"We try harder"	Doyle Dane Bernbach	1963
11.	Federal Express	"Fast talker"	Ally & Gargano	1982
12.	Apple Computer	"1984"	Chiat/Day	1984
13.	Alka-Seltzer	Various ads	Jack Tinker & Partners; Doyle Dane Bernbach; Wells Rich, Greene	1960s, 1970s
14.	Pepsi-Cola	"Pepsi-Cola hits the spot"	Newell-Emmett Co.	1940s
15.	Maxwell House	"Good to the last drop"	Ogilvy, Benson & Mather	1959
16.	Ivory Soap	"99 and 44/100% Pure"	Proctor & Gamble Co.	1882
17.	American Express	"Do you know me?"	Ogilvy & Mather	1975
18.	U.S. Army	"Be all that you can be"	N.W. Ayer & Son	1981
19.	Anacin	"Fast, fast, fast Relief"	Ted Bates & Co.	1952
20.	Rolling Stone	"Perception. Reality."	Fallon McElligott Rice	1985
21.	Pepsi-Cola	"The Pepsi generation"	Barton, Durstine & Osborn	1964

Source: http://adage.com/century/campaigns.html

No.	Company	Campaign	Agency	Year
22.	Hathaway Shirts	"The man in the Hathaway shirt"	Hewitt, Ogilvy, Benson & mather	1951
23.	Burma-Shave	Roadside signs in verse	Allen Odell	1925
24.	Burger King	"Have it your way"	BBDO	1973
25.	Campbell Soup	"Mmm mm good"	BBDO	1930s
26.	U.S. Forest Service	Smokey the Bear/ "Only you can prevent forestres"	Advertising Council/Foote, Cone & Belding	
27.	Budweiser	"This Bud's for you"	D'Arcy Masius Benton & Bowles	1970s
28.	Maidenform	"I dreamed I went shopping in my Maidenform bra"	Norman, Craig & Kunnel	1949
29.	Victor Talking Machine Co.	"His master's voice"	Francis Barraud	1901
30.	Jordan Motor Car Co.	"Somewhere west of Laramie"	Edward S. (Ned) Jordan	1923
31.	Woodbury Soap	"The skin you love to touch"	J. Walter Thompson Co.	1911
32.	Benson & Hedges 100s	"The disadvantages"	Wells, Rich, Greene	1960s
33.	National Biscuit Co.	Uneeda Biscuits' Boy in Boots	N.W. Ayer & Son	1899
34.	Energizer	The Energizer Bunny	Chiat/Day	1989
35.	Morton Salt	"When it rains it pours"	N.W. Ayer & Son	1912
36.	Chanel	"Share the fantasy"	Doyle Dane Bernbach	1979
37.	Saturn	"A different kind of company, A different kind of Car."	Hal Riney & Partners	1989
38.	Crest toothpaste	"Look, Ma! No cavities!"	Benton & Bowles	1958

Source: *http://adage.com/century/campaigns.html*

39.	M&Ms	"Melts in your mouth, not in your hands"	Ted Bates & Co.	1954.
40.	Timex	"Takes a licking and keeps on ticking"	W.B. Doner & Co & predecessor agencies	1950s
41.	Chevrolet	"See the USA in your Chevrolet"	Campbell-Ewald	1950s
42.	Calvin Klein	"Know what comes between me and my Calvins? Nothing!"	CRK Advertising	1981
43.	Reagan for President	"It's morning again in America"	Tuesday Team	1984
44.	Winston cigarettes	"Winston tastes good--like a cigarette should"	William Esty Ad Agency	1954
45.	U.S. School of Music	"They laughed when I sat down at the piano, but when	Ruthrauff & Ryan	1925
46.	Camel cigarettes	"I'd walk a mile for a Camel"	N. W. Ayer & Son	1921
47.	Wendy's	"Where's the beef?"	Dancer-Fitzgerald-Sample	1984
48.	Listerine	"Always a bridesmaid, but never a bride"	Lambert & Feasley	1923
49.	Cadillac	"The penalty of leadership"	MacManus, John & Adams	1915
50.	Keep America Beautiful	"Crying Indian"	Advertising Council/Marstellar Inc.	1971
51.	Charmin	"Please don't squeeze the Charmin"	Benton & Bowles	1964
52.	Wheaties	"Breakfast of champions"	Blackett-Sample-Hummert	1930s
53.	Coca-Cola	"It's the real thing"	McCann-Erickson	1970
54.	Greyhound	"It's such a comfort to take the bus and leave the driving to us"	Grey Advertising	1957

Source: *http://adage.com/century/campaigns.html*

55.	Kellogg's Rice Krispies	"Snap! Crackle! and Pop!"	Leo Burnett Co.	1940s
56.	Polaroid	"It's so simple"	Doyle Dane Bernbach	1977
57.	Gillette	"Look sharp, Feel Sharp"	BBDO	1940s
58.	Levy's Rye Bread	"You don't have to be Jewish to love Levy's Rye Bread"	Doyle Dane Bernbach	1949
59.	Pepsodent	"You'll wonder where the yellow went"	Foote, Cone & Belding	1956
60.	Lucky Strike cigarettes	"Reach for a Lucky instead of a sweet"	Lord & Thomas	1920s
61.	7 UP	"The Uncola"	J. Walter Thompson	1970s
62.	Wisk detergent	"Ring around the collar"	BBDO	1968
63.	Sunsweet Prunes	"Today the pits, tomorrow the wrinkles"	Freberg Ltd.	1970s
64.	Life cereal	"Hey Mikey"	Doyle Dane Bernbach	1972
65.	Hertz	"Let Hertz put you in the driver's seat"	Norman, Craig & Kummel	1961
66.	Foster Grant	"Who's that behind those Foster Grants?"	Geer, Dubois	1965
67.	Perdue chicken	"It takes a tough man to make tender chicken"	McCabe, Sloves	1971
68.	Hallmark	"When you care enough to send the very best"	Foote, Cone & Belding	
69.	Springmaid sheets	"A buck well spent"	In-house	1948
70.	Queensboro Corp.	Jackson Heights Apartment Homes	WEAF, NYC	1920s
71.	Steinway & Sons	"The instrument of the immortals"	N.W. Ayer & Sons	1919

Source: http://adage.com/century/campaigns.html

No.	Brand	Slogan	Agency	Year
72.	Levi's jeans	"501 Blues"	Foote, Cone & Belding	1984
73.	Blackglama-Great Lakes Mink	"What becomes a legend most?"	Jane Trahey Associates	1960s
74.	Blue Nun wine	Stiller & Meara campaign	Della Famina, Travisano & Partners	1970s
75.	Hamm's beer	"From the Land of Sky Blue Waters"	Campbell-Mithun	1950s
76.	Quaker Puffed Wheat	"Shot from guns"	Lord & Thomas	1920s
77.	ESPN Sports	"This is SportsCenter"	Wieden & Kennedy	1995
78.	Molson Beer	Laughing Couple	Moving & Talking Picture Co.	1980s
79.	California Milk Processor Board	"Got Milk?"	Goodby Silverstein & Partners	1993
80.	AT&T	"Reach out and touch someone"	N.W. Ayer	1979
81.	Brylcreem	"A little dab'll do ya"	Kenyon & Eckhardt	1950s
82.	Carling Black Label beer	"Hey Mabel, Black Label!"	Lang Fisher & Stashower	1940s
83.	Isuzu	"Lying Joe Isuzu"	Della Famina, Travisano & Partners	1980s
84.	BMW	"The ultimate driving machine"	Ammirati & Puris	1975
85.	Texaco	"You can trust your car to the men who wear the star"	Benton & Bowles	1940s
86.	Coca-Cola	"Always"	Creative Artists Agency	1993
87.	Xerox	"It's a miracle"	Needham, Harper & Steers	1975
88.	Bartles & Jaymes	"Frank and Ed"	Hal Riney & Partners	1985

Source: http://adage.com/century/campaigns.html

89.	Dannon Yogurt	Old People in Russia	Marstellar Inc.	1970s
90.	Volvo	Average life of a car in Sweden	Scali, McCabe , Sloves	1960s
91.	Motel 6	"We'll leave a light on for you"	Richards Group	1988
92.	Jell-O	Bill Cosby with kids	Young & Rubicam	1975
93.	IBM	Chaplin's Little Tramp character	Lord, Geller, Federico, Einstein	1982
94.	American Tourister	The Gorilla	Doyle, Dane Bernbach	L a t e 1960s
95.	Right Guard	"Medicine Cabinet"	BBDO	1960s
96.	Maypo	"I want my Maypo"	Fletcher, Calkins & Holden	1960
97.	Bufferin	Pounding heartbeat	Young & Rubicam	1960
98.	Arrow Shirrs	"My friend, Joe Holmes, is now a horse"	Young & Rubicam	1983
99.	Young & Rubicam	"Impact"	Young & Rubicam	1930
100.	Lyndon Johnson for President	"Daisy"	Doyle Dane s	1964

Source: *http://adage.com/century/campaigns.html*

✠✠✠

Global Quiz Bank

−Gladys Ambat

Demy Size • Page: 256
Price: ₹ 120/- • Postage: ₹ 20/-

Quiz blitzkrieg are brain fitness fundas of a unique kind! The thrill to win or lose gaming session of a quiz programme can give you an optimum level of mental fitness and alertness. You simply bubble over with the sheer joy of challenge.

The book is a lively presentation for all youngsters and a pleasant leisure companion for the elders. The veteran author has put together over 4000 exciting quizzes and interesting brain-teasers to get all keyed up. While you race through every page — you could find yourself sitting on the edge of the chair. Yet, you get charged with a spirit of challenge to unearth hidden answers or solve uncharted problems by your latent thinking power. The enormous variety of startling quizzes promises to stretch your mind to new horizons of thought and learning. This is your vantage point for self-improvement and an enriching pursuit.

The book covers:

- Quiz Medley & Quickies
- Palindromes & Proverbs
- Villains in History & Fiction
- Word Game — A Bouquet of Words
- Vowel-less Words & Words of Two Letters
- Sobriquets & Scrambles

The list has 163 subtitles, each crammed with many interesting quizzes and teasers. Read on and get ready for action to star in a captivating quiz gaming session.

QUIZ TIME

–Ivar Utial

Demy Size • Page: 127
Price: ₹ 120/- • Postage: ₹ 20/-

Enliven your leisure hours with Quiz Time! It guarantees you to give many hours of exciting mind storming quiz games. Excel your ability to hold social meetings with charisma and quiz gaming. This book employs tested quiz skills in very well-defined structure for easy comprehension. The book is aimed to cater to a large section of the society.

Mind Benders
Brain Teasers & Puzzle Conundrums

– Vikas Khatri

Demy Size • Page: 152
Price: ₹ 110/- • Postage: ₹ 20/-

* Enjoy mental workouts?
* Like numerical brain teasers?
* Dabble in solving puzzles?
* Use maths occasionally?
* Accept intellectual challenges?
* Love solving Riddles?

Answer "YES" to any of these questions, and this is the right book for you!

If you want to test your logic skills and have fun, then read this collection of brain teasers and mind benders and check out how smart you are!!

Count the Cubes

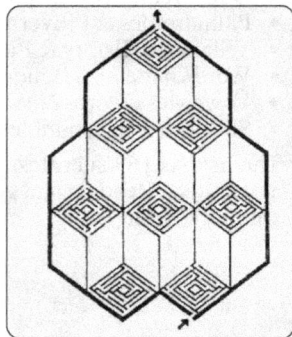

SCIENCE QUIZ BOOK

–Rajeev Garg & Amit Garg

Demy Size • Page: 192
Price: ₹ 96/- • Postage: ₹ 20/-

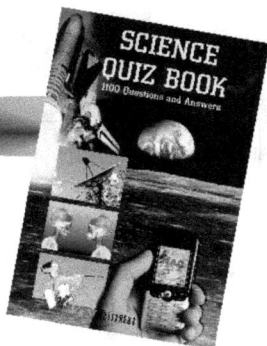

That is what your child will find in this A to Z Quiz Series — brilliant books brimming with the latest information and simple explanations of fascinating facts and feats about our constantly evolving world.

Designed to boost your child's knowledge base, each page comes alive with new facts in an engrossing form of short Questions and Answers with explanatory illustrations, all of which makes it easy to read, easy to follow and easy to remember.

Each book covers a subject comprehensively. Innumerable students, parents and teachers have found these books helpful in boosting the knowledge level of children. These books come in handy for quiz contests, competitive exams, admission tests, career development etc.

The best feature about these books is that they do not look or read like standard textbooks. Therefore, studious as well as not-so-studious children enjoy reading them and imbibing information contained in these pages. In fact, the A to Z Quiz Series makes learning so much fun that you will wonder why you never gifted your child a set before!

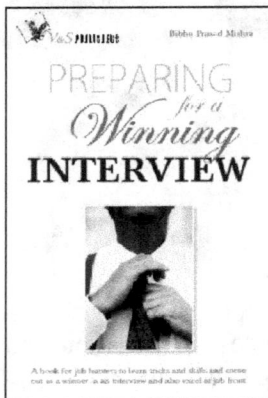

Author: Bibhu Prasad Mishra
Format: Paperback
Language: English
Pages: 223
Price: ₹ 150
Publishers: V&S PUBLISHERS

Author: Barun Roy
Format: Paperback
Language: English
Pages: 124
Price: ₹ 150
Publishers: V&S PUBLISHERS

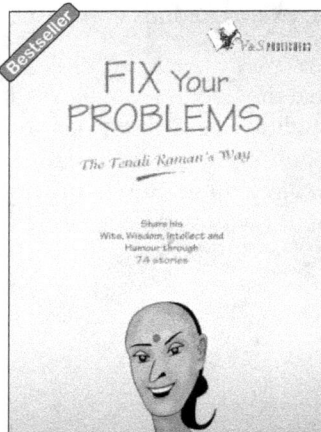

Author: Vishal Goyal
Format: Paperback
Language: English
Pages: 224
Price: ₹ 150
Publishers: V&S PUBLISHERS

www.ingramcontent.com/pod-product-compliance
Lightning Source LLC
Chambersburg PA
CBHW070358270326
41926CB00014B/2608